FREDERICK THE GREAT
AND THE MAKING OF PRUSSIA

"The King Flute Player." Painting of Frederick the Great by Jean Léon Gérôme (1824–1904). *(Three Lions)*

FREDERICK THE GREAT AND THE MAKING OF PRUSSIA

Edited by **THOMAS M. BARKER**
State University of New York at Albany

HOLT, RINEHART AND WINSTON
New York • Chicago • San Francisco • Atlanta
Dallas • Montreal • Toronto • London • Sydney

Cover illustration: Death mask of Frederick the Great.
(German Information Office)

CONTENTS

CHRONOLOGY

THE HOUSE OF HOHENZOLLERN
IN THE SEVENTEENTH AND EIGHTEENTH CENTURIES

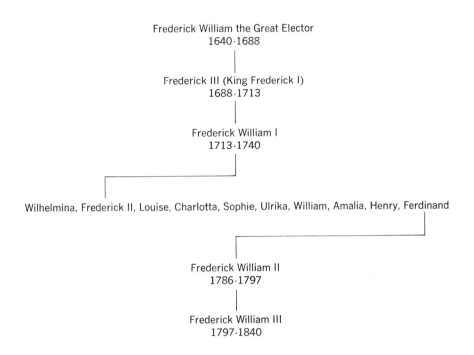

Frederick William the Great Elector
1640-1688

Frederick III (King Frederick I)
1688-1713

Frederick William I
1713-1740

Wilhelmina, Frederick II, Louise, Charlotta, Sophie, Ulrika, William, Amalia, Henry, Ferdinand

Frederick William II
1786-1797

Frederick William III
1797-1840

THE HOUSES OF HABSBURG AND LORRAINE
IN THE EIGHTEENTH CENTURY

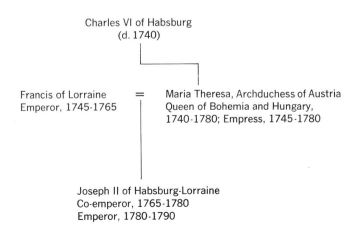

Charles VI of Habsburg
(d. 1740)

Francis of Lorraine   =   Maria Theresa, Archduchess of Austria
Emperor, 1745-1765   Queen of Bohemia and Hungary,
                                1740-1780; Empress, 1745-1780

Joseph II of Habsburg-Lorraine
Co-emperor, 1765-1780
Emperor, 1780-1790

"Austria" was not a legally valid geographical designation for all the Habsburg domains until 1804 but rather the name of the dynasty itself, the so-called "Casa d'Austria." Before that time the word was used in an official sense mainly to indicate the two provinces of "Austria Above and Below the Enns," or "Upper and Lower Austria" as they have been known more recently.

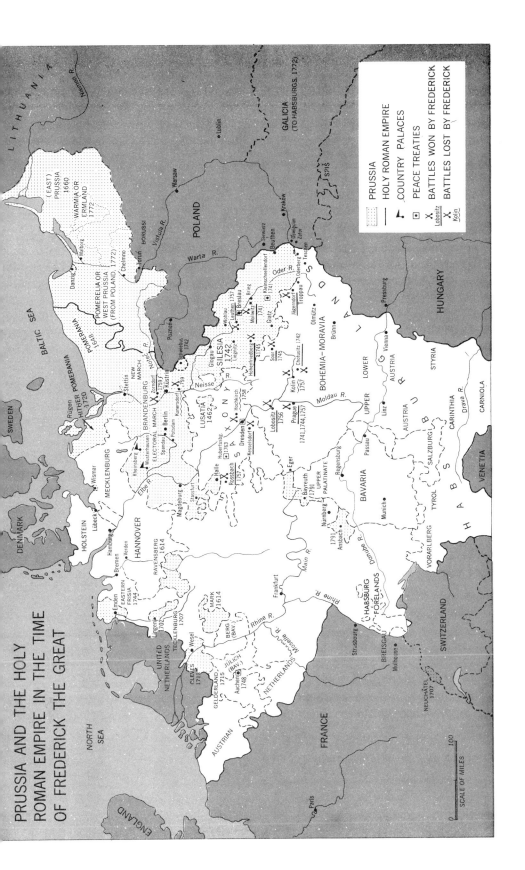

PRUSSIA AND THE HOLY ROMAN EMPIRE IN THE TIME OF FREDERICK THE GREAT

Legend:

- PRUSSIA
- HOLY ROMAN EMPIRE
- COUNTRY PALACES
- PEACE TREATIES
- Lobositz ✗ BATTLES WON BY FREDERICK
- Köln ✗ BATTLES LOST BY FREDERICK

SCALE OF MILES
0 · · · 100

INTRODUCTION

As a result of two world wars precipitated by rampant German militarism, the adjective Prussian has acquired an opprobrious connotation in the vocabularies of other nations. Moreover, the validity of Hohenzollern traditions has come into question even in Germany itself, both after 1918 and since 1945. In seeking to explain the tragic history of recent decades many writers, learned and popular, point to the authoritarian and martial traits of the Prussian-colored, German national character. Inevitably, one of the main targets is the figure and reign of Frederick the Great (1740–1786), who, it is generally agreed, raised his country to great-power status not only in the Holy Roman Empire but throughout Europe. To be sure, the eighteenth-century ruler has had to share the burden of censure with more remote protagonists like Martin Luther or with more modern scapegoats like Bismarck and Nietzsche. It has also become apparent that completely abstract factors such as Romanticism and its offshoot, the "folkish" movement, have had a detrimental influence upon German development.[1]

There is something unique about Prussia's Enlightened Despot. The idiosyncracies and mysteries of Frederick's personality, the dramatic quality of his military and political deeds, the novelty of royal participation in the cultural activity of the Age of Reason, and his concern for the material welfare of his people were features that captured the imagination of contemporaries and assured the permanent interest of posterity. Already as a youth Frederick was the focus of international attention. The poor relationship between the Crown Prince and his rigid, doctrinaire sire, Frederick William I, was a matter of common knowledge at other European courts, which sought to exploit the situation for their own benefit. A sensational escape attempt of the heir to the throne and his close friend Hans Hermann Katte (1704–1730) was brutally punished by the reigning monarch and became the scandal of the decade. Ultimately there was a reconciliation of sorts, and the future sovereign was permitted enough leisure to indulge his belletristic interests seriously. His delightful country villa at Rheinsberg became a cosmopolitan intellectual retreat, a miniature colony of scholars

---

[1] See George Mosse, *The Crisis of German Ideology: The Intellectual Origins of the Third Reich* (New York: Grosset & Dunlap, 1964). Available also as a Universal Library paperback.

1

and artists. The idyll lasted until the death of Frederick William I in 1740. Thereupon the curious European public suffered a severe shock.

The sudden demise of the last male Habsburg, Charles VI, was followed by Frederick's swift lunge into Austrian Silesia. No one had expected the effeminate Hohenzollern dilettante to seek glory on the battlefield. Even more astonishing was the fact that he became a superb general, a peer of Caesar and Gustavus Adolphus. Fellow Europeans also marveled when the veteran of many campaigns sheathed his sword and resumed his wide-ranging intellectual pursuits, the most brilliant of which was a tumultuous association with Voltaire. Equally novel was Frederick's fervid devotion to the practical arts of peace, to the tasks of domestic reform. Wonder was transformed into admiration and respect, although frequently mixed with fear and hate, when this pacific interlude was interrupted by a new clash of arms. The incredible trials which the royal *philosophe* underwent and survived in the Seven Years' War were without parallel in human memory. During the final twenty-three years of his life Frederick's presence seemed to hover over the Continent, austere and remote, yet somehow benevolent and reassuring, a symbol of stability and order.

In light of such a career it is hardly surprising that Frederick has been the object of a century and a half of scholarly dispute and that the discussion has been as sharp as the debates over Metternich and the Iron Chancellor. In Germany the reaction of the earliest professional historians was relatively favorable although quite varied.[2] Leopold von Ranke, a Thuringian-born Prussian scholar who matured intellectually between 1815 and 1845, examined French archival materials and came to regard the Hohenzollern monarch as the creator of a kind of Berlin-Vienna axis. He viewed this dual power system ("German Dualism"), a characteristic of the internationalist age which he himself knew so well, as a blessing. Hence Frederick, even when behaving atrociously, was expressing deeper, nonpersonal moral and spiritual values. Two other classical German pedagogues, the abstruse and obscure Johann Gustav Droysen and the broadly influential popularizer of power politics Heinrich von Treitschke studied the same documents as von Ranke but drew different conclusions. They judged the Friderican era from the standpoint of "Little German" *(kleindeutsch)*, or Prussian-dominated, nationalism. Of course, in time there was also a "Greater German" *(grossdeutsch)*, or pro-Austrian, reaction. The first representative of the Habsburg cause was an embittered Hannoverian exile in Vienna, Onno Klopp, a prolific writer on many diverse historical subjects. He damned Prussia's ruler as the spoiler of Germany, an outlook that was later shared by native Austro-German nationalists.

The nineteenth century also produced other, more conceptualized interpre-

---

[2] Bibliographical references to most of the historians discussed in the following three paragraphs will be found in Suggestions for Further Reading (under "Older or Historiographically Significant Accounts") at the end of this volume.

tations of "Old Fritz." The Hegelian view of human experience as an ideological process was given a new twist by the pioneer philosopher of history Wilhelm Dilthey. A firm believer in constitutional monarchy, he maintained that Frederick was a good example of mankind's self-conscious moral autonomy. No sovereign incorporated the primacy of the intellect better than Prussia's royal *philosophe.* Dilthey's attitude is crucial because it appears to have strengthened the abstract analytic framework within which many twentieth-century German historians have continued to function. Highly subjective thought still characterizes their work. Another Bismarckian period writer, the rigidly Marxist Franz Mehring, reacting to the revisionist Socialism of his day, saw Frederick's reign as a manifestation of the automatic operation of economic laws. Mehring, too, created a historiographic tradition and has had disciples in more recent times. His views are essential to German Communism.

French opinion on the subject of Frederick the Great has oscillated considerably. The great republican historian Jules Michelet applauded him as an enemy of the hated *ancien régime,* but France's defeat in 1870–1871 led the Duc de Broglie to denounce the patron of Voltaire as the founder of a militarist state. More recent Gallic scholarship has been less partial.[3] British historiography has produced two trends. Thomas Carlyle is responsible for the hero-image of Frederick in the English-speaking world, although he built upon a positive public reaction from the time of the Seven Years' War when Prussia was Britain's only major ally. Thomas Babington Macaulay, a champion of early nineteenth-century liberalism and Carlyle's prime impetus for writing, could hardly describe an absolute ruler without expressing some distaste. This bias, reinforced by the experience of two great wars, has tended to predominate in both semipopular and learned accounts.

By the end of the last century the discipline of history was firmly grounded and possessed a relatively sophisticated methodology. Generally speaking, scholarship from this period on is not merely a chapter in the history of ideas but retains practical value for study and research. It is significant that the personality of Frederick the Great, the subject of the first group of selections, became the initial object of attention in this newer era of learning. The Frenchman Ernest Lavisse, perhaps the most eminent historian of the first decades of the Third Republic, made a major contribution to the subject by exploiting the techniques evolved by the social sciences during his own lifetime. He applied psychological analysis, albeit somewhat primitively, in his discussion of Frederick's youth, which seemed to him to provide the key to the man's puzzling dual nature in the post-1740 years. Lavisse emphasizes the lasting effects of the insensate military regimen imposed upon the Crown Prince by his father.

Almost forty years later Arnold Berney too sought to understand Frederick within a developmental context. Berney, Jewish but not unaffected by either

---

[3] Especially Pierre Gaxotte. See Suggestions for Further Reading.

German nationalism or the traditional German romantic taste for pseudometaphysical language, sought to produce a new and definitive biography but failed to finish it, thanks to Hitler. Only one volume was published, and its appearance as late as 1934 was a minor miracle. (The author's tragic destiny raised also the subsidiary question of the contributions of "non-Aryans" to modern German intellectual life and of their integration into an industrialized and urbanized social environment.) The book's chief theme is Frederick's internal, spiritual evolution. There is stress upon the relationship between his early maturing need for self-fulfillment and intellectual factors. Personality growth is presented not as an example of the innate audacity of a hero but as a unique instance of autodidactics.

Among critics of the German past in the post-World War I era was the literary titan Thomas Mann. His concern for the negative aspect of German history is reflected in the work of the gifted essayist and popular biographer Ludwig Reiners. Through him we view Frederick's personality in the isolation of old age. While Reiners evokes an underlying sense of tragedy, he is above all impressed by what he feels are "demonic-ghostly" character features. The contradictions are so crass that ultimately it is impossible for another human mind to penetrate their meaning, and so Frederick remains an enigma.

The puzzling nature of Frederick's personality was evident to his contemporaries. His youthful rebellion and the philosophical-literary activity at Rheinsberg, which included publication of his tract ostensibly *against* the ideas of Machiavelli, would scarcely have led people of the time to expect so "Machiavellian" an action as the invasion of Silesia in 1740. The controversy over this issue, the focus of the second group of essays, has never ceased. Reinhold Koser's massive biography, still the basic factual summary, treats this problem on the basis of an intimate knowledge of massive documentary records. However, Koser was a son of Wilhelminian Germany. Although he sees Frederick as a mere dynast motivated primarily by interests of the Prussian state and although he is not uncritical in certain respects, he tends to vindicate royal actions, thereby revealing his own latent patriotism.

Heinrich Ritter von Srbik likewise treats the Silesian question from a nationalistic vantage point, but his interpretation is colored by the "Greater German" political philosophy. For this outstanding modern Austrian historian it was tragic that Prussia's sovereign and Maria Theresa, rulers of the elder twins among the sibling states of the Empire, came to blows over the rich eastern province. He saw the struggle as basically fratricidal and hence injurious to all members of the German family of states.

For the late, long-lived G. P. Gooch, the "Dean of British historiography," the problem of Silesia was relatively simple: Frederick was completely unscrupulous and perpetrated a raw, indefensible act of aggression. The suspicion naturally arises that Gooch, at least in this respect, stands in the shadow of his earlier compatriot Macaulay. The judgment, in the selection included here, is clearly moralistic even if the author is more sparing of condemnation in his other fine essays on various aspects of Frederick's reign.

The second great issue of political morality in the career of Prussia's ruler is his share of responsibility in the First Partition of Poland (1772), a joint enterprise of Prussia, Russia, and Austria, presented in the third group of essays. The distaste of Poles for both Germans and Russians—old Austria no longer exists—continues to be a basic fact of political life in Eastern Europe. Poland, it should be recalled, was dissected not only on three occasions during the eighteenth century but also at the Congress of Vienna and in 1939. The culmination of its neighbors' brutality was reached in Nazi policies toward a "racially inferior" people and in a Soviet mass execution of bourgeois nationalist officers (the Katyn Massacre), not to mention the Red Army's failure to aid the Warsaw Rising of 1944. Thus Frederick's role in the initial destruction of Polish rights remains topical.

Otto Hintze, one of the more productive German scholars of the first several decades of the twentieth century, expresses a revealing opinion on this subject. References to Hintze's various monographic studies abound in contemporary historical literature, and so there can be little question that his total accomplishments were substantial. Nevertheless, he too was a product of Wilhelminian nationalism, even more so than Koser. Hintze's analysis of the Polish question, presented in a survey treatment of the Hohenzollern dynasty that appeared not long after the outbreak of World War I, makes some points which are still valid. Yet ethnocentric attitudes are so much in evidence that one is tempted to ask whether historians of his ilk do not bear some responsibility for the shaping of public opinion in modern Germany and hence also for the organized criminality which Eastern Europe suffered between 1939 and 1944.

Of course Hintze must not be regarded as an archetypal figure. There were others in his profession whose outlook was more liberal and humanistic. After the Versailles Treaty many of them, like the novelist Mann, began to take new stock of their past. The traumatic experience of defeat led to a reexamination of national history in the search for an explanation. One of these critics was the political and intellectual historian Friedrich Meinecke, who had begun to develop his basic frame of reference prior to 1914. He now refined his concept of history as a struggle between a crude, unprincipled striving for state power—*raison d'état,* or "Machiavellism"—and the august, philanthropic force of conscience.[4] (Sometimes the phrase *"Kratos versus Ethos"* is used to describe this clash of opposites.) On balance, Meinecke, who lived on after World War II to expound an even dimmer view of German history,[5] concluded that Frederick had yielded to the more primordial instincts within the body politic even if the

---

[4] Friedrich Meinecke, *Machiavellism* (London: Cambridge University Press, 1955). Available in the United States as a Yale University Press hardcover and as a Praeger paperback.

[5] Friedrich Meinecke, *The German Catastrophe* (Cambridge, Mass.: Harvard University Press, 1950).

good—his domestic reforms—coexisted with the evil. Meinecke's ideas about reason of state were highly influential, but since they were so fresh, they were also subject to elaboration by others.

The most talented of the historians directly under Meinecke's gigantic influence was Gerhart Ritter, who construes Frederick's behavior as a more personal version of *raison d'état,* as a disciplined, rationalized form of power politics. (Ritter elsewhere attributes this virtue to Bismarck, probably incorrectly.) Scion of a pastoral family, conservative and old-fashioned in outlook, he admires Frederick's commitment to the traditional values of sobriety, economy, duty fulfillment, and devotion to collective welfare. He downplays the relationship of these factors to the Enlightenment and argues that they stem mainly from the prior history of Brandenburg-Prussia and the historical example of the French monarchy. Because of his own high moral standards Ritter could only regard Hitler as utterly reprehensible. His Friderican biography, published in 1936, is surely a subtle criticism, by way of comparison, of the *Führer* and his new barbarism. Yet he is somewhat equivocal in his attitude toward the Polish issue. It appears as if his somewhat antiquated cast of mind—he also tended to ignore the results of more recent social science research—sometimes hobbled his judgment.

In sharp contrast to the elegantly formulated views of Ritter, a generalist, is the solid, straightforward work of a young American specialist, Herbert H. Kaplan. Kaplan underscores the role of Frederick's brother Prince Henry, who was eager to aggrandize the Prussian state and was prepared to share hegemony in Central Europe with Austria. Initially reluctant, Frederick finally came to favor partition, justifying his decision as preservation of the balance of power and citing arguments that appear to have been advanced originally by Henry.

A far more fundamental question than either the invasion of Silesia or the partition of Poland concerns the basic nature of the state over which Frederick presided. More precisely, what were the political dynamics that underlay Prussia's expansion? Why was Frederick driven to rule in what seems to be so arbitrary and aggressive a fashion? What were the intangible forces that impelled him? Meinecke was the first to broach this problem systematically. Ritter pursued it not only in his biography of Frederick but also in a massive study published after World War II, the purpose of which was to trace the influence of militarism in German life. Despite terrible personal experiences during the Hitler period, Ritter did not discard his earlier interpretation of Frederick but merely broadened its foundations after taking some account of the progress in historical research during the intervening period.[6] Frederick remains more or less a hero

---

[6] Ritter based his later views upon a fuller understanding of the pre-1740 past of Frederick's life and laid greater stress upon the role of the Christian-influenced, moral tradition of Early Modern territorial absolutism in the development of a specific Prussian *raison d'état* (see *Staatskunst und Kriegshandwerk* [Munich: Oldenbourg, 1954] p. 25 ff.). He also recognized a greater affinity between the French Enlightenment's advocacy of an ethical employment of reason and Frederick's own outlook (*ibid.,* p. 335). Nonetheless he held that the Prussian monarchy continued to be marked by "the same [unique] system of a strictly rational self-limitation of power" and found support for his view by a "close observance of the military and foreign policy of the Friderican state" (*ibid.,* p. 40).

figure. The appearance of *The Art of State and the Craft of War,* as the work was called, aroused a major scholarly controversy. The eminent diplomatic historian Fritz Fischer took serious exception to much of its contents.[7] Ludwig Dehio, then editor of *Historische Zeitschrift,* Germany's chief historical journal, also protested vehemently. The result was to give new impetus to a discussion of the subliminal facets of Friderican politics, the subject of the fourth group of selections.

The terms of the debate have tended to remain intangible, abstract, and, in fact, sometimes almost unreal. Dehio, chronicler of the European balance-of-power struggle, accepts the premise of *raison d'état* as a major element in the historical process, as does Ritter, the object of his attack. Yet he not only reaffirms Meinecke's negative judgment of Frederick but goes further: the Prussian monarch is a prime example of untrammeled militarism with all its horrifying consequences for succeeding generations.

Ritter's essential conservatism does not lack defenders, however. Walther Hubatsch replied to Dehio in a short essay which offers yet another solution to the problem of stately dynamics. Hubatsch, too, proceeds on the basis of *raison d'état* but in a much more complex fashion than any of his predecessors. He perceives in Frederick the Great a peculiar manifestation of the Age of Reason. Enlightenment features are related to the institutional history of the Early Modern Period, in particular to the slow development of a special brand of princely Absolutism in the Hohenzollern territorial state of the sixteenth and seventeenth centuries, a phenomenon much illuminated by the research of recent decades. Frederick is a blend of the philosophical-literary milieu of his own day and of the traditions of pre-1740 Prussia, an Enlightened Despot *sui generis* and a highly original expression of the reason of state principle.

The materialist approach to understanding the past which reaches back to Marx and his various predecessors, the focus of the last group of selections, continues to be relevant, whether open-minded or dogmatic in form. The German-American scholar Hans Rosenberg, not bound by the stringent guidelines imposed upon historians by the East German government, takes a comprehensive, interdisciplinary approach which involves history, political science, and sociology as well as economics. He asserts that the basic character of the Prussian state was shaped by the growth of an originally bourgeois, later ennobled bureaucracy, a German version of the French *noblesse de robe,* which gradually evolved into a socioeconomic interest group linked to some extent with the existing landed aristocracy. Frederick's particular role was simultaneously to impede and promote the fusion of the two components of the resultant élite. This body, which developed its own *espirit de corps,* was harnessed to the service of a militaristic monarchy. Frederick's less-gifted successors lost control over the whole apparatus; herein lies the tragedy of German history.

In the German Democratic Republic orthodox Leninist-Stalinist doctrines—

---

[7] Author of *Germany's Aims in the First World War* (New York: Norton, 1967; also a Norton paperback), which makes the Berlin government appear as the chief aggressor of the 1914–1918 period.

doctrines of economic determinism—provide the basis for all instruction and research. Prior to about 1952 there was little concern for German history as such, but from that date on there has been a deliberate effort to stimulate "patriotic consciousness, above all of the working classes as the main source of national strength." One of the chief architects of this so-called "national viewpoint toward history" was the Viennese-trained political scientist and old-time Party stalwart Dr. Leo Stern (from whom the quotation stems). An important practical step in the implementation of the official creed was the establishment in 1958 of the *Deutsche Historikergesellschaft,* the stated task of which is to "rally the historians of the German Democratic Republic active in research, teaching, and popular scientific work in order to apply and disseminate dialectical and historical materialism in all areas of the science of history." The East Germans have shown special interest in the peasant risings of the Early Modern Period, the domestic reforms of the Napoleonic era, the Wars of National Liberation, and radical democratic participation in the struggle for German unification.

A particularly prominent figure in recent years has been Gerhart Schilfert, who has addressed himself to the Friderican question among other things. His royal subject, the traditional father-figure of all Germans, is not easy to handle, given the presuppositions. Frederick, portrayed as a tool of the Junker class, emerges as a kind of antihero who delayed the operation of immutable historical laws and was thus a factor in the sad fate of a more recent Germany. This analysis, much of which is borrowed directly from Mehring, is worth considering. There is a growing tendency among Western historians, in part because of Rosenberg's work, to appreciate the influence of class interests in the development of capitalism.

It is striking that the lifetime of Frederick the Great coincided with the formation of an intellectual environment that still prevails. Despite frequent disenchantment with its efficacy, Western man still has faith in the power of reasoned dialogue. Frederick's career also paralleled the rise of a more general consciousness of history. A study of scholarly viewpoints concerning the expansion of Prussia should illustrate not only how the vision of the past has evolved in the years since his death in 1786 but also how this process has reflected the lasting influence of the ideological presuppositions of the age in which he lived. Each generation of researchers and commentators has sought to apply the technique of rational discourse to its analysis of the Friderican era. The results are often highly differentiated and permeated with the concerns of the authors' own times. This is inevitable and even desirable because thereby future students are bequeathed the challenge of revision and reinterpretation. The contrast of views and the hope of finding an explanation closer to the reality of the past may well be the traits from which the craft of history derives its special charm.

In the reprinted selections footnotes appearing in the original sources have in general been omitted unless they contribute to the argument or better understanding of the selection.

ERNEST LAVISSE (1842–1922), professor at the
Sorbonne and École Normale Superièure, was the
inventor of collective historical studies, a genre in
which Frenchmen have shown particular skill. He may
be considered one of the great synthesizers of the new
disciplinary knowledge of the nineteenth century. His
chief published work is a still basic, multivolume
Histoire de France. The inquiring nature of his mind
is evident also in his astute, psychologically oriented
investigation of Frederick the Great's youth. The
following passages derive from the core chapter and the
conclusion of this work.*

Ernest Lavisse

An Unstable Childhood

In March of 1724 Frederick William I
and his son graciously deigned to attend
a reception given by General von Grumb-
kow, one of the chief ministers of the
Prussian Court. Pointing to the Crown
Prince, the King suddenly said: "I would
like to know what goes on in this little
head. I know that he does not think the
way I do. There are people who are giving
him ideas different from mine and incit-
ing him to criticize everything. They are
scoundrels." He repeated his words and,
turning to his son, added: "Listen to what
I am telling you, Fritz. Always keep an
efficient, large army. You can have no
better friend, for without it you will be
lost. Our neighbors would like nothing
better than to trip us up. I know their

intentions, and you too will get to know
them eventually. Believe me, do not
waste your time on vanities. Concentrate
on reality. Have a good army and money.
They are the foundation of a prince's
glory and security." He then gave the
boy a few raps on the cheek, light blows
that were destined to become ever more
vigorous and ultimately turn into beat-
ings.

At the moment of this first sign of discord between father and son, the Crown
Prince was twelve years old. The misunderstanding was already complete, and
it was public knowledge. The foreign
diplomats informed their courts about
the incident and commented upon the
King's words in their dispatches.

*From Ernest Lavisse, *La Jeunesse du Grand Frédéric* (Paris: Hachette, 1894), pp. 134–141, 443–447.
Translated by Thomas M. Barker.

Frederick's delicate nature could not tolerate his father's forceful manner. The King so exhausted and harrassed him that the child, his back hunched over, had the air of an old man, a veteran of many campaigns. The King wished to accustom him to hardship. Any indication of weakness or sensitivity enraged the royal taskmaster. He made a terrible scene when he saw the boy take gloves along on a hunting trip at a time when the temperature was well below freezing. On another occasion he chose the horse that Fritz was to ride. The groom noted that the animal was difficult to manage. The King cut him short. As the party was leaving Potsdam, a gust of wind ripped off His Majesty's chapeau, causing the Crown Prince's horse to take the bit in his teeth. The boy was quick-witted enough to slip out of his stirrups and throw himself to the ground. However, he hurt his knees, thighs, and neck. The handle of his sword gashed his sides so badly that he bled copiously. When they returned to the palace, the Queen cried and sobbed. The King was exasperated and ordered his son to appear the next morning at the changing of the guard. The heir to the throne did as he was commanded although badly injured and unable to slip his hands through his body coat.

The Crown Prince was inclined toward elegance, the comforts of life, and magnificence. He scarcely enjoyed the means to satisfy these tastes, but he did what he could. He did not like to eat with the double-pronged iron forks which were customarily employed in German taverns and which resembled a primitive weapon. The King surprised him one day using a three-pronged silver fork. He was caned.

If some kind spirit had accorded Frederick William three wishes on the day his son was born, the King would not have hesitated in making his choice: "Let my son be a good administrator, a good soldier, and a good Christian." But Fritz showed no interest at all in thriftiness. The King wanted his heir "to keep count of his ducats," as he himself had once done, and demanded such extreme accuracy that the Queen was quite beside herself, disturbed to see the boy "tight-fisted at so tender an age." However, Fritz let others perform this task for him. He refused to learn how "to make a return on his money." Moreover, he was selfless, generous, and charitable. During a trip he had just made, the city of Magdeburg gave him a gift which, according to custom, was due any heir to the throne visiting the town for the first time. He refused to accept it. Compelled by his father to do so, he announced that he would keep the money until his own accession in order to distribute the sum among poor people burdened with taxes. The city of Stassfurth wished to "honor his passage with 200 ducats." He ordered that the cash be given to the poor and forbade his governors to utter a word about his generosity to the King.

Fritz did not like soldiers. He found them crude and ridiculous, and preferred in place of their company that of men "who know something." He made generals the butts of his practical jokes. One day, in Westphalia, he dined with the King at Rosendaal Castle as the guest of General von der Mosel. The plan was to go hunting after the meal. The old general, who had drunk more than he should have in order to be gracious, tried to hoist himself into the saddle, but the Crown Prince had deliberately shortened his stirrups, taking great delight in the ensuing scene. While the King was himself quite fond of pranks, he believed that they should be perpetrated upon scholars and teachers.

Would Fritz remain a good Christian? The learned Professor Francke [a cleric] as upset about this after his visit to Wusterhausen, for in the midst of general enthusiasm over his arrival Frederick would not even talk with him. "One could almost say," the poor man wrote in his journal, "that something is bothering His Highness." Only on the fifth day did the Crown Prince summon the worthy theologian, receiving his compliments with ill-humor and limiting himself to eight words. Francke was expecting thanks for having sent the heir to the throne certain edifying tomes, but it was the governor who expressed gratitude, whereupon the youth left the room. The next day at dinner, the King being absent, Francke noted that Frederick was regarding him scornfully during a conversation about ghosts. As the group rose to leave, the cleric heard the future ruler remark in a loud voice: "Right there is someone who believes in them." Francke then learned that the evening before the castellan of Wusterhausen, a pious man, had chanced upon the Crown Prince, who inquired where the official was taking the lamp he held in his hand. "To the Professor, Your Highness," he replied. "Then," Frederick answered, "a pharisee is about to meet a pharisee, for he is a pharisee like you." The man of God, now very concerned, vowed to pray for the royal prodigal. Certainly Fritz badly needed someone to pray for him. He was inclined "by nature to all the sciences" but neglected divine knowledge. He was supposed to be confirmed in April 1727, and the rite was actually performed on schedule. But so that Frederick would be ready in time, the Court pastor found it necessary to double the hours of instruction. His governors were forced to admit to the King that for six months their charge had been avoiding his religious studies.

Neither a good steward nor a warrior nor pious, the Crown Prince was destined to trouble the soul of his father deeply. . . . It would have been a miracle had Frederick William not permitted himself to be carried away by his own inherent tendency toward violence. He began with mild slaps that became firmly delivered strokes. He chastised Fritz because of the hunting gloves and because of the three-pronged fork. As the King himself was punctilious and went to extremes in everything he did, he quickly drove his son to despair. The child from whom the monarch had expected filial devotion, tender respect, and absolute confidence, little Frederick, or "Fritzchen," seemed like a rebel and also dangerous. The French envoy, noting the "alienation of King and Prince," feared that "things may go too far." Indeed, Prussia's sovereign was already comparing his eldest born unfavorably with the younger [Augustus] William. The brother received all the tenderness the father could muster. At dinner he let William say grace. Bowed and with hands clasped, he remained standing behind the little boy. If the child was ailing, he covered him with kisses. He stopped the infant whenever he came upon him, picked him up and caressed him "for a full fifteen minutes." He said, "I would not wish to wager large odds on any of my children over the others, but (pointing to little William) I have real confidence in this one. He has a good character. I warrant that he will become a decent person." It is possible to surmise that already at this date, three years before the tragic Katte affair,[1]

---

[1] Hans von Katte (1704–1730) was Frederick's close friend. When the King's savagery became absolutely unbearable, the two youths attempted to run away, but they were caught, thrown into prison, and charged with desertion. Both were court-martialed. Katte was beheaded in Frederick's presence, causing the Crown Prince to lapse into unconsciousness. The heir to the throne was kept in jail for some time but ultimately pardoned, partly because of the moderating influence of royal advisers. In the meantime

Frederick William could not prevent himself from thinking that his kingdom would be well provided for if he were to place it in the hands of a younger son who promised to become a man of principle. He could no longer bear even the sight of the eldest. From that point on the life of the family became intolerable. A kind of terror swept through the royal household. The Queen cried all day long. It was even painful to look into the face of the Crown Prince. Everyone took note of the "dark melancholy" in his eyes. He admitted his unhappiness to friends, and his letters expressed his distaste for life. He apologized to a sick friend, Lieutenant von Borcke, for not being able to distract him: "Rather I myself need to be diverted so that my spirits can recover." He begged the young officer not to die: "Death is the thing I fear most for those who are close to me, but I fear it least for myself."

At court and throughout the kingdom opinion favored the highly intriguing victim as opposed to his father. In fact it appeared as if the Crown Prince had committed no other crime than to be unlike his sire. . . . This prosaic man who desired to lock up a twelve-year-old in the world of "reality," who wished to deny him the right to admire and love anything outside the military and administrative realms, this brute who struck and injured his son because of trifles, had about him the air of a maniac and abominable tyrant. Yet one could not let the matter rest there if one wished to be entirely just and to apportion to each of the principals his share of responsibility in the coming tragedy.

First one must look beyond father and son, study the milieu in which Frederick

was raised, the influences to which h• was subject; then one must scrutinize hi actions, question his motives, probe from the very moment of its first developmen the true nature of his personality, which was more complex than his father's. The King said that there were people who were giving him ideas different from hi own. Who were they?

. . . Without wishing to, Frederick' teachers inculcated him with ideas and intellectual habits quite contrary to the royal example. The child's instincts re acted strongly in response to their efforts. For his part he added to assigned reading others that were forbidden. His mind thus became accustomed to dwelling in an at mosphere quite different from the one before his eyes. There was no one like Frederick William in [Fénelon's] *Télé-maque* or in the novels of chivalry. The heavy drinkers, tobacco smokers, and sword swingers of Potsdam and Berlin seemed singularly coarse compared with the philosophers of antiquity or with adventuresome and gallant knights. Still, Frederick was not educated solely by professors. At their side, as pedagogical and inspirational influences, were two persons whom he loved and by whom he was loved most tenderly, namely, the Queen and the elder of the two princesses, Wilhelmina. . . .

Frederick grew up in a strange environment, amidst a tumultuous clash of base passions, in the company of ministers and servants who had sold themselves to foreign masters, in an atmosphere of shady deals, spying, and intrigue, in the filthiness of a Court where [despite everything] the King himself was perhaps the only decent person. The Crown Prince did not feel out of place. He managed to conduct himself quite adeptly in a slough of corruption and ended by being more skilled than his competitors. In the crisis of

---

he had made up his mind to conform outwardly to the King's will and accordingly served the administrative and military apprenticeships that were subsequently demanded of him.—Ed.

narriage he alternated between clever
ies and bold truth.[2] Surely the tyranny
f his father and the detestable example
f a malevolent entourage tended to de-
ase him. Yet nature had predestined him
o great dexterity in the art of duping
one's fellowmen.

He was so dissimulating that he hid
rom everyone another, more intrinsic
rederick—the personality his father so
notly desired and would have adored. He
alled his uniform a shroud. When Frederick William forced him to learn the
rade of prince in the Demesnal Chamber
crown lands administration] at Küstrin,
he affected such a zeal for outrageous
expressions in his letters that the King
could only conclude that he was a perfect
hypocrite. . . . The truth, which was to
appear later, was that he was an excellent
colonel who kept his regiment as well as
did anybody else. It was as if the military
lessons of Major Senning had been presented to the mind most capable of appre-
ciating, understanding, practising, and
surpassing them. It was as if "the young
clerk of Küstrin had quickly grasped

all there was to learn about good business
management." He was certain that he
possessed the knowledge of how to govern, and he already dreamed of applying
it to the detriment of others. He saw ahead
of him a rich future of politics and war,
the whole of his reign and an ample destiny for Prussia. . . .

The resemblance to a father whom he
rejected and from whom he concealed
his true being would rise to the surface
when he himself was master of the land.
Frederick William I was contained within
Frederick II, but Frederick II possessed
a genius which his progenitor lacked.
. . . He was intelligent and had a taste
for belletristic and philosophical subjects.
The muses charmed and consoled him,
made him think about life in the manner
of an ancient sage. They added to his
strength of soul. We have perceived in
this strange young man a mixture of
epicureanism and stoicism which was
destined to recur in the King and which,
along with his genius, princely virtues,
faults and vices, scorn for all law, per-
fidious cynicism, intellectually grounded
humanitarianism, and the inhumanity
that is essential for leaders of men, was
the stuff of which the historical figure
of Frederick the Great was made.

---

[2] Frederick was compelled to marry (1733) Elizabeth Christina of Brunswick-Wolfenbüttel, a kind,
good, and patient but relatively uneducated and
simple-minded person.—Ed.

ARNOLD BERNEY (1897–1943) was a student of the Freiburg economic and constitutional historian Georg von Below. His first study as a young scholar treats Frederick William I's relationship to the Habsburgs. Influenced also by Meinecke, Berney next set out to d⟨o⟩ a full-scale Friderican biography. He only managed to reach 1755, for after the Nazi seizure of power German academic life was "coordinated" and Jewish careers ended. The *Historische Zeitschrift* was no longer able to publish a review of the book. Foreign reaction was mixed. W. F. Reddaway, sensing the patriotic undertones of the developmentally conceived work, expressed reservations,[1] but Walter Dorn thought that the volume and its publication under such conditions constituted an encouraging sign.[2] The student may wish to ask what Berney's fate says about the role of Jewish intellectuals in modern Germany.[*]

Arnold Berney

Self-confirmation and Historical Fulfillment

The ruler ... rebelled against the thinker, the statesman against the *philosophe*. In the world of action the fortuitous decay of stately, national, and human existence was a question that had no validity. There, as Frederick saw matters, only courageous persistency and bold planning, the restless striving and the political or martial deeds of kings made any sense. Great men were the yardstick of present and future events. They endured beyond the narrow confines of individual life and became part of the more sublime essence of states and nations. *Vis-à-vis* their political omnipresence, the history of rulers and states became a kind of court in which sovereigns and monarchies were subject to judgment. And so, in his mind's eye, he saw Richelieu and Mazarin looming up as the controlling impulse behind Louis XIV. Tilly, Montecuccoli, and Prince Eugene bestirred themselves to oppose the tired and fruitless policies of the last Habsburg [Emperor Charles VI]. Gustavus Adolphus and Charles XII mournfully regarded the decline of Sweden as a great power. The voice of the great Prince of Orange sounded a warning note against the hesitant, dependency-prone policies of a latter-day Netherlands.

---

[1] *English Historical Review*, LI (1936), 177.
[2] *American Historical Review*, XL (1934–1935), 329–330.

---

[*]From Arnold Berney, *Friedrich der Grosse: Entwicklungsgeschichte eines Staatsmannes* (Tübingen: Verlag von J. C. B. Mohr, 1934), pp. 270–273. Translated by Thomas M. Barker.

Meanwhile, behind Frederick II there appeared the electors and kings of the House of Brandenburg: the contentious, imperially oriented, territorial princes of the sixteenth and early seventeenth centuries; the mighty phenomenon of the Great Elector, savior in the midst of wartime suffering and want, champion of a new unity for the state's ultimately enlarged territories, founder of the army and a great commander who "never abused his heroic virtues . . . ," the disciplined and industrious but kind-hearted and sociable Frederick William; and, last of all, Frederick's own late father, described with forebearance and respect but not without noting failures in foreign policy, a ruler whose magnificent domestic achievements his son was fully able to appreciate only now in the decade of peace.[3] Frederick saw all these ancestors engaged in a continuous struggle, both covert and open, as protagonists of liberty and growing statehood against the "despotism" and "arrogance" of the House of Habsburg. He considered all of them, not because of polished theory but on the basis of sheer dynastic existence and political intent, as the disciples and perfectors of that interpretation of the imperial constitution developed during the seventeenth century by Hippolythus a Lapide and Sammuel von Pufendorf.[4] They all sprang to their feet behind the King to warn and encourage him, to tolerate some actions and demand others. They aligned themselves along the highroad of his career. They shadowed him in his constantly shifting efforts to increase the importance and the power of the House of Brandenburg and in his striving, through accomplishment, deeds, and success, to become worthy in his own right of princely status. When Frederick considered the relationships and the conflicts within the European political system, he felt himself to be on the side of the soaring angels, the victors, of growth and expansion. Here it was, then, that contemplation of the fates and the attempt to comprehend the history of states and nations ceased; here it was that the world of the present, self-awareness and the sense of mission in his own royal life, commenced.

The phrase with which Frederick[5] most sharply delineated the heroic example of the Great Elector [1640–1688], making him stand out from the figure of Louis XIV [1643–1715], had a prophetic tone: "The German hero did more; he blazed a trail all by himself." No less portentous was Frederick's praise of manly steadfastness, soldierly imperturbability, unfearing decisiveness and his admiration of courageous death in either war or peace—all expressed in numerous utterances from this period. More clearly than in the labyrinth of foreign policy or in the manifold, laborious, and ultimately unsuccessful "intrigues" of his reign, his written words reflect an extreme patriotic readiness for great deeds, a will for comprehensive statesmanly and soldierly self-confirmation. Here was foreshadowed the ripeness of human, and hence statesmanly, vitality from which the greatness of Frederick II issued and from which it drew its timeless strength.

---

[3] Prussia dropped out of the War of Austrian Succession (permanently) in 1745 and enjoyed relative peace and security until the Diplomatic Revolution of 1756, the starting point of the Seven Years' War. —Ed.

[4] These men, primitive yet learned and perspicacious political scientists, tended to stress the sovereignty of the individual territorial states within the Empire.—Ed.

[5] The reference here is to Frederick's own historical authorship. Quotations in the text are phrases that he used and which are quoted in this work or taken from other writings.—Ed.

This process of maturation culminated in the ability to stand, fight, and endure, entirely alone, in the physical world. The King found no help, support, no salvation in God. He never doubted the existence of an almighty and supreme Being. But he knew that this Essence "owed" nothing to man. He doubted that Divinity intervened to alleviate human misery; he did not believe that the weak voice of man could echo so far. He heard the buzzing of eternity prior to birth and after death. From this he took the measure of the nothingness and perfect mortality of human life. In the gigantic order of things—established in overwhelming and inexplicable fashion by the heavens—the Empire, the state, individual human beings vanished. All of them sank into the shades of the universe, between those worlds without number "that swim in empty space around their suns."

Frederick once labeled himself a pagan. But he was not a pagan as a consequence of religious kinship with pre-Christian antiquity, with primeval Germany, Rome, and Greece. Spiritual sacrifice and prayer were foreign to him. His life dispensed with that sacral element which is appropriate when one is faced with a God who actually rules. He was a pagan in the sense of Christian tradition, a naysayer to dogmas of redemption. He admitted his skepticism with uncharacteristic, almost melancholy earnestness. He realized how significant a decision had to be made here. He had chosen between affirmation and negation in a Scriptural sense: "for Holy Writ proclaims that God spues the lukewarm from His mouth" [Rev. 3–16].

But God's great distance from man did not beget emptiness or doubt, did not cause despair and collapse. The powers of a life lived but once shone forth in the full brilliance of their transitory beauty. For the sake of his own unique being, his possession alone, a state should rise to its fullest perfection, a people should be brave and virtuous, a ruler inexhaustible and self-sacrificing. On earth all being must obey the law of necessary self-realization. In this existence all questions concerning the hereafter are irrelevant. In the realm of politics it is a matter of "indifference" whether or not a ruler is religious. Frederick the Great regarded unfettered, autonomous self-realization of the state as the most important vital process, and he pursued this goal to perfection by means of his own singularly exemplary service.

This service was not the kind that Zarathustra woefully decried. It was not slavishly subordinated to the overhasty opinions of the easily manipulated masses. It was rooted in the selectivity of a passionate talent for rulership and in the powerfully prevailing self-discipline of a monarch who through restless self-education, indefatigable intellectual schooling, and a constantly nagging dissatisfaction with himself sought to be worthy of his exalted office; who measured all his decisions by the political standard of existential necessity, securely rooted geographically and historically in space and in time; who simultaneously exerted himself to satisfy his subjects' need for "happiness" and "well-being" by both arbitrary and mild leadership, with either didactic or indulgent compassion. Frederick wanted a greater and a mightier Prussia, but he was no conqueror. He demanded the greatest possible achievement and most exacting service from his Estates and subjects, but he was no tyrant. He maintained, enlarged, and educated the finest army in the West, but he despised the reckless use of military resources as a degrading game with military pawns. He wished to ensure a broadly influential, honorable, and pacific existence for his north German kingdom by all the planning techniques of domestic and foreign power politics. In the midst of this ceaseless striving he became the most kingly of men. His royal office became the incarnation of just and honorable, chivalric and bold rulership, a monarchy regarded with the greatest hostility by the rest of Europe, a new creation capable of further German growth, far distant from the ancient, evanescent Empire—a kingship courageously conscious of the judgment of great men and all righteous-minded mankind.

The conceptual as well as the realized figure of the "great ruler" had both natural roots and a supranational effect. It originated with the early Enlightenment's view of the state. It was also thought of, visualized, and yearned for in Germany and in other Occidental countries. Yet it was realized for the first time—and quite alone—by Frederick II in Prussia. It therafter reacted upon the world with new validity. To be sure, by language, descent, and culture the great King was by no means just a typical German, but the actual statesmanly, heroic radiance of this human phenomenon sprang from the most sacred recesses of the German spirit. His royal person, subsisting in a sense of responsibility to the state and reflecting a highly intrinsic, almost mechanistic awareness of obligation, was akin to the purest and noblest features of the German character, as manifested by his political-intellectual discipline and triumphant spiritual fortitude. Within this German rulership, which had reached maturity more through discipline, endeavor, and achievement than by blood, habit, or tradition, there slumbered the power without which it would have been impossible to bear the fateful blows of the Seven Years' War, the power from which the "steadfastness of long life" flowed and with which the self-fulfillment and self-consummation of more advanced age became possible.

LUDWIG REINERS (1896–1957) was an active figure in German literary circles. In numerous essays and longer works he combatted bigotry and prejudice. He tried to present the results of learned investigation in semipopular form and to promote a humanistic view of existence. His exquisitely composed portrait of Frederick owes much to the somber ruminations of Thomas Mann, who was much perturbed over the course of German history and had begun to probe its meaning, including Frederick's reign, even before 1914. Reiners is, of course, no professional scholar, and there are certain, lesser factual errors in his study. Yet its sensitivity and philosophical perspective can be valuable to historians.*

Ludwig Reiners

An Insoluble Riddle

From now on he was known as "Old Fritz," a horrible name if one has a feeling for horror. And, indeed, it is truly most horrible when a demon becomes popular and receives a nickname.

—Thomas Mann

The old man had gotten up at four in the morning, had read the incoming mail, dictated several dozen answers and glosses, horsewhipped a lackey for having admitted some female into the palace, and worked for three hours on an essay entitled "In Praise of Inertia." He had then ridden out to inspect the troops, had kept to the saddle for two hours, had received some foreign visitors, and now sank clumsily into his chair at the dinner table. His gout was causing him terrible pain. He was wearing the uniform of the First Infantry Guards Regiment. From a few, remaining patches of the original material it was possible to see what the color had once been. The tassles on his dagger were faded. The formerly black, now yellowed high boots were held together at the top with string. In the opinion of his visitors the sash around his chest must have been a relic from the days of his accession to the throne. The jacket cuffs he obviously used to wipe off his pen. From his pocket he pulled

*From Ludwig Reiners, *Friedrich* (Munich: Verlag C. H. Beck, 1952) pp. 322–333. Translated by Thomas M. Barker. An English edition of this work, translated and adapted from the German by Lawrence P. R. Wilson and entitled *Frederick the Great*, was published in 1960 in England by Oswald Wolff (Publishers) Ltd. and in the United States by Putnam's Sons.

two snuffboxes filled with Spanish tobacco. Their diamond-studded covers contrasted strangely with his miserable garb. He began to sniff. His clothing was proof that he had been doing this all day long, and a few stains on his red-brown face seemed to be several days old. The seventy-two-year-old monarch peered suspiciously across the table. He then dipped his fingers into the soup bowl and plucked out a piece of meat, placing it on the tablecloth so that it would cool off for the greyhound waiting at his feet. He noted how astonished his visitors were at his careless behavior, and how they stared at his small bent figure in its shabby uniform. So as to shock them even more he took a pair of scissors from his pocket and trimmed his nails. Then, as was his habit, he mixed champagne with coffee and began to speak.

At this moment everything that was odd and puckish about the man vanished as far as his audience was concerned. He spoke in a lively manner, with engaging sprightliness and very much to the point. All his sentences were balanced and well-knit. Nothing was unclear. Everything was full of sparkling wit and imagination. The tenor of his voice was soft, his gestures graceful. His guests had expected a misanthrope and had found him to be absolutely charming. He talked of art, war, medicine, literature, religion, philosophy, ethics, history, lawmaking, about the great age of Augustus and of Louis XIV, about the sociability of the ancient Greeks, the candor of Henry IV, the renascence of the sciences, the aberrations of Voltaire, the chivalry of Francis I, the domineering character of President Maupertius [of the Prussian Academy], and the imaginary illnesses of his friend d'Argens. He related anecdotes from time to time, the same ones he had used to impress Katte fifty years earlier. He car-

ried on for five hours and only occasionally encouraged his table partners to ask brief questions.

At five P.M. he rose from his chair to give instructions to a young diplomat about to leave for Turkey as his minister. A clerk was summoned, and the King began to brief the new envoy about the purpose of the mission, the interests of Prussia and other powers, and the character and constitution of Turkey. Then he began to dictate the instructions. At the end of every paragraph he paused, provided clarifications and at the same time played with the greyhound, which had jumped into his lap. After he had allowed the young man himself to speak in order to determine whether the royal will had been properly understood, he continued to dictate and fondle the dog. And so the interview proceeded until two sheaves of instructions were filled. At no point did he ask the clerk to repeat what he had dictated. Despite all interruptions he had not lost the thread of his thought. Then [his cabinet secretary] came in and asked for signatures. [The foreign secretary] had forwarded a difficult note from England because he knew of no answer that would not embarrass Prussia. Such problems were trifling for Frederick. "I want nothing to do with this," he wrote back. "Make up an answer, Austrian style. Use ingratiating but thoroughly vague terminology, which means neither yes nor no but is simply incomprehensible." Then he went into his bedroom—he never ate supper—undressed by himself, drew up a scruffy sable pelt and fell asleep about nine.

The annual routine of Frederick's life was no less uniform. One could predict what he would be doing each day of the year: "It seemed as if his will had command even over strictly physical things, for if he lay ill in bed prior to scheduled revues and journeys, when day broke he was better and did what he had planned." Between Christmas and January 22 he was in Berlin to preside over the great holiday receptions. Even the Queen caught a glimpse of him. On January 23, the day before his birthday, in order to avoid being congratulated, he drove off to Potsdam with a sigh of relief. He had a dromedary loaded down with his snuffboxes precede him, as if he wished to emphasize the legendary features of his character. In April he went to Sans Souci, where military inspections were beginning. In May he regularly visited Pomerania and West Prussia, but he never traveled to East Prussia because the nobility there had paid homage to the Empress Elizabeth during the Seven Years' War. In June he was in Magdeburg, and after that the state budget was worked out. The month of August belonged to Silesia. In September there were maneuvers, and in November he returned to Potsdam.

His environment had become lonely. "I work, take walks and see nobody," he occasionally remarked. When he met his wife for the first time in seven years, his greeting consisted of a single sentence: "Madame has become more corpulent." He presented her to his sister Ulrika with the words, "This is my old cow whom you already know." He forgot his golden wedding anniversary. He also despised most other members of his family. He considered the successor to the throne indolent and extravagant: in all likelihood Prussia would no longer exist thirty years hence. His brother Henry hated him, especially because Frederick had banished his lover, a certain Herr von Kaphengst. All the monarch's friends were gone: they were either dead or in exile. General von Seydlitz had succumbed to syphilis. To be sure, Frederick

was not particularly fond of this all-too popular man, who responded in kind when made fun of. Other friends like his reader H. A. de Catt and General Lentulus had married, much to the King's annoyance. He had had a falling out with his daily companion Colonel Guichard otherwise known as Quintus Icilius. This officer had wanted to marry a young noblewoman, and the King had refused to grant his bourgeois comrade the necessary permission "because, to tell the truth, he is of too poor extraction." The stubborn-minded man resigned from the army and married anyway. Even his reinstatement failed to revive the old friendship fully. Baron Pöllnitz, one of the most willing butts of the King's jokes, managed to hold out for a long time. "Tell me, what was the name of the chap to whom you sold the fake silver in The Hague?" the King was accustomed to ask him at dinner. Or else the poor wretch was offered a hundred talers if he would change his religion a second time. Finally he too died, "regretted by nobody but his creditors," according to Frederick. The person whom the King missed most of all was the Marquis d'Argens, to whom he had addressed all his spiritual effusions while on campaign. To cap the relationship, the Prussian ruler presented his confidant with a beautiful bookcase filled with leather-bound editions of all the Church Fathers, the Marquis' favorite reading, but unfortunately when d'Argens flipped open the volumes, he discovered that they contained only blank paper. The seventy-four year old nobleman was no longer fully able to appreciate practical jokes, and in a humble letter asked for permission to spend his last days in his Provençal homeland. Having been forewarned by Voltaire's fate, he immediately returned all the letters he had received from the King. Frederick was indignant: "I must confess that Frenchmen manage to outdo just about any tomfoolery that I could expect of them. They used to come to their senses when they were thirty years old; now there is no particular age limit. However, you may do what you like, Monsieur Marquis. You strengthen me in my long-held conviction that princes exist on earth only to reap ingratitude." The old man had hoped in vain to find peace under the southern sky. Frederick had a fictitious episcopal encyclical circulated in his former friend's native county, in which d'Argens was condemned as an atheist. It closed with the phrase: "Finally, dear brothers, I implore you, by the Lord's most profound mercy to pursue this godless person eagerly and energetically. His extinction will bring about the end of our cares and effect Heaven's blessings." In a letter which the Marquis wrote shortly before his death he reproached the King for having mistreated a selfless admirer.

In everyday life, too, Frederick displayed a masklike harshness. When he dismissed a servant despite a plea for mercy on bended knees, the fellow went to his room and put a bullet through his head. "Where did he get hold of a pistol?" the King asked. "I should not have expected so much courage of him."

Apart from the King himself, the dinner time atmosphere was like that of a Trappist monastery. His only remaining friends were his dogs, who slept in his bed at night and lay at his feet on pillows during the day. When he was traveling, he kept himself informed of their illnesses through daily couriers, and when the animals died he had them laid out on a bier and solemnly carried into a crypt.

He bitterly missed intelligent friends. Conversation was a vital necessity for him. When d'Alembert stated, upon inquiry, that the King of France had never spoken with him, Frederick responded, "But with whom does he talk then?" Yet the royal *philosophe* refused to remain in Berlin as President of the Academy. The echo of Voltaire's footsteps still bothered him. Thus he had to satisfy himself with quite ordinary people. One of his visitors reported that the King said one day, "'I have summoned both of you to me because I am too sick to participate in conversation myself. . . . My head is so dizzy that I hardly know where I am. So please chat with one another as if I were not here. Talk about whatever you want. I will listen to you if I am strong enough. This will distract me, at least for a little while.' But we did not guide the conversation for very long. The King quickly took over, and the Colonel and I were no more than an audience. Although the King suffered great distress, at least occasionally, he alone spoke until after nine o'clock. About every quarter hour he interrupted himself, overcome by his pains. He then called his servants and had them administer a spoonful of some kind of medicine. After this he would ask us where he had stopped and go on with the discussion."

To be able to speak in front of other human beings was absolutely necessary for the old man. When his eighteen-year-old nephew Henry died—whom he had loved like a son—he composed a eulogy which his reader Thiebault was supposed to pronounce in the Academy. But first the King read it aloud himself. "To begin with he spoke like somebody who is trying to control himself. One noticed this by the tone of his voice, which he tried to make firm. He spoke slowly and made frequent, rather long pauses. But already by the second or third page his voice began to quiver. Tears rose to his eyes. He frequently had to draw his breath and reach for his handkerchief. He wiped his face, coughed, cleared his throat. Despite all this he was unable to reach the end of the fourth page. His eyes were brimful of tears. He could no longer see, and his choked and weakening voice became inaudible. With a sob he could no longer restrain he stretched out his hand to me and silently passed on the manuscript." In old age the King even learned to show indulgence. When a lady of his court had an illegitimate child, he wrote, "This is a quite ordinary experience. There is no court, not even a nunnery, where something like this doesn't happen. I, who have so much indulgence for the weaknesses of my own sex, am the last person to cast stones upon maids of honor who become mothers. They procreate the human race instead of destroying it as do those raw and bloodthirsty politicians with their accursed wars. I must confess to you that I am infinitely more drawn to such affectionate souls than to those chastity dragons who continually backbite their fellow women, or those contentious females who are fundamentally evil and malicious. Let the child be carefully educated, do not permit a family to be dishonored. Have the poor girl removed from court without notice or annoyance, and spare her reputation as much as possible."

In the depth of his being Frederick was softer than he wished to appear. When he declaimed his favorite verses from Racine's *Britannicus* concerning the duty of princes and the happiness of subjects, tears always came to his eyes. Gradually, as a result of the "floggings which he imparted to his soul," the epicurean delight in life which characterized the Crown Prince evolved into the granite-like face of the old King. Yet he never lost his yearning for the esthetic world or for the peace of his study chamber.

He who was admired by all Europe for his unexampled steadfastness groaned in desperation, "I do not possess the spirit of greatness." To be sure, he had managed to wipe out the stains of the degradation suffered during his childhood, but nobody knew how much the effort had cost him. Receptive to pleasure but fully conscious of the troubles that lurked threateningly on the horizon, he had chosen to enter upon the path of glory, regardless of danger and sacrifice. However, along this fearful trail his whole environment and all mankind had become for him mere objects of ratiocination and rhetoric, or at best of unfeeling action, a form of behavior the result of which would clearly be negative in human terms. He once assured an astonished visitor that since he himself was more sensitive than others, he had also experienced more pain. When Ulrika lost her husband, he wrote, "Dear sister, one surely deceives one's self if one expects to find more good than bad in this world. It is the worst of all possible worlds. Fleeting moments of relaxation are one's only happiness. My life has been nothing more than an interweaving of unpleasantness, suffering, and misery."

All his scorn for mankind and the world notwithstanding, he was occasionally inclined to become almost effervescent and to look at the human condition through rose-colored glasses. "Life, my dear Darget [another reader]," he wrote on . . . New Year's Day, 1768, "is a dreadful thing when one grows old. One must decide either to perish on the spot or to watch one's self die slowly, bit by bit. But despite all this there is a way to be happy. One must rejuvenate one's self with ideas, ignore the body, maintain an inward cheerfulness until the final act of the drama is played out, and strew the last few steps along the road with flowers." "His joyous temperament came from his superiority over other human beings," said Catherine the Great, the most perspicacious of his contemporaries. An unimpeachable witness, the French *philosophe* Claude Helvetius, reported that when the old man wanted to he could be as charming as Voltaire, and many of his visitors remarked that he was able to put everyone at ease. Unlike most rulers, he viewed life from a detached and distant vantage point. Therefore he did not lack a sense of irony either. "Many thanks, dear child," he wrote to his niece, "for the kind words you have addressed to your old uncle. But he doesn't deserve them. He is a decrepit, old gossip whom one must send to the world beyond as quickly as possible. There he can continue to talk drivel. But I know that you don't think this way. Your feeling heart has sympathy for the old skeleton because it is your relative and because you wish good to everyone from the depths of your own innate goodness. As long as I live, I will love you and give you all my affection." Indeed, he was often able to regard even his own lifework with ironic distance. Once when heraldry was being discussed, he suggested a thundering Jupiter for Austria, the pirate chieftain Mercury for England, the star of Venus for France, and "for us an ape because we ape the great powers without being one."

This irony was also revealed in many of the King's decrees and marginal comments. Once a colonel shot a stag in a royal hunting preserve and had to pay a fine of a hundred talers. The officer begged that he be kept in his sovereign's good graces. Frederick scribbled on the margin of the document, "This makes no difference at all; for such a price many other stags are at his disposal." A high-ranking bureaucrat wished to requisition twenty-four horses for a business trip. Frederick: "With that number of animals

one can pull twenty-four cannon. An administrator is not important enough to merit employment of such heavy transport. Let him have eight horses, and if he gains weight, eight to ten."

A Jew complained that his rabbi had refused to let him shave off his beard. Frederick: "The Jew Posener should leave his beard and me unshorn."[1] Several doctors were competing for the job of official examiner in Lebus. Frederick decided in favor of the one "who is most humane and has killed the least number of people." A young theology student applied for a pastoral post. Frederick wrote, "Second Samuel, Chapter 10, Verse 5." (The last part of this passage reads, "Tarry at Jericho until your beards be grown . . ."). A congregation asked for another pastor because the current one did not believe in the Resurrection. Frederick: "The pastor stays. If he does not want to get up at the Last Judgment, he can stay in bed." The presbytery of a Potsdam church requested that reconstruction work be halted because completion of the work would deprive the church of light. Frederick: "Blessed are they who do not see and still have faith."

A soldier had stolen coins from an image of the Mother of God and maintained that the Virgin Mary had brought the money into his quarters in response to prayer. The King inquired of Catholic clergymen whether such a miracle was possible and then wrote on the dossier, "The alleged malfeasant is not to be punished, first, because he continues to deny the theft and, secondly, because the miracle which has occurred is not impossible according to the theologians of his Church. However, for the future I forbid

---

[1] The German phrase *"ungeschoren lassen"* means both to "leave unshaved" and to "leave (somebody) in peace."—Ed.

him under threat of severe punishment to accept anything more from either the Blessed Virgin or any other saint." The story has a genuine Friderican sound, but unfortunately it is apocryphal.

There can be no question about the King's crudity. He was unable to suppress any kind of brutality if it seemed funny to him. An artillery lieutenant, the bastard son of a noble-born colonel, asked to be legitimitized. Frederick wrote on the margin, "Am I supposed to naturalize every son of a bitch?" When a pastor requested that his daughter be provided for, Frederick replied, "These priests' daughters, why don't the sluts get married? If they are infirm, we can take care of them. But if they are healthy, they should either work or be married. For that is appropriate to their status."

For the most part such observations were translated into chancellery German by the royal secretaries. Still, Lessing was absolutely correct in saying, "God has no sense of humor and kings shouldn't either. For if a ruler does happen to have a sense of humor, who will protect us from the danger of his passing unjust sentence simply because he is able to make a successful pun?"

The demonic-ghostlike aspect of the King's character; the unsettling mixture of harshness and delicacy, misanthropy and humanitarianism, willingness to help and malevolence, devotion to duty and cynicism, literary activity and skill in the governmental arts: how did all this come about? The terrible humiliations he suffered as a youth, the public dishonor he had to undergo—perhaps these were memories he wished to observe with a nimbus of glory. When one considers how fantastically difficult it must have been to overcome such a childhood emotionally, it is no wonder if demons dwelled in his soul. His uncontrollable predilection for the crassest forms of

speech and for sharp and cynical phraseology may also stem from this source. Similarly, he was disgorging existential dregs accumulated while his terrible fate unfolded.[2] He despised the world and mankind because he had been treated despicably.

The twisted quality of his personality may also derive from other, equally profound depths. Many contemporaries passed on the story that the King loved his own sex. His stubborn avoidance of his wife, his malignant hatred of everything feminine, his preference for handsome pages, his denial of female company to his lackeys, the remnants of his correspondence with his valet M. G. Fredersdorf: all these facts tend to confirm the rumors. There can be no evidence for this in the documents, however. Everyone kept silent in the face of an absolute monarch. One of the few who was independent and bold enough to speak openly, Voltaire, reported details. Frederick's last doctor, Johann Georgvon Zimmermann, maintained that the ruler had been operated upon during his youth because of venereal disease and suffered lasting genital damage as a result. Allegedly for this reason, he never let himself be seen naked in the presence of his lackeys even when he was ill. Voltaire implied similar things. Whoever wishes to may also conclude that the King's gigantic energy represented an effort to overcome feelings of inferiority: he wanted to show the world he was really a man. Yet all these reflections fall into the category of supposition. Such a personality will always remain a riddle.

A German historian referred a critic of the King to the royal death mask saying, "If you ever look like this, then you may pass judgment."

---

[2] The reference here is to the ghastly trials of the Seven Years' War. — Ed.

REINHOLD KOSER (1852–1914) belonged to that generation of historians who first undertook the massive task of systematically publishing archival materials and thus of providing a theoretically sound basis for interpretive judgment. In 1874 he was entrusted by the Prussian Academy with the editing of Frederick's correspondence (see Suggestions for Further Readings). In 1890 he became professor of history at Bonn University and in 1896 Director of the Prussian State Archives. From 1905 until his death Koser was also board chairman of the *Monumenta Germaniae Historica*. His extensive biography of Frederick remains indispensable, its use only slightly impaired by a mild patriotism. Both features—documentary orientation and a nuance of personal approbation—stand out in the following description of the background to the involvement in Silesia.*

Reinhold Koser

Carpe Diem, *or Prussia's Self-interest*

Brandenburg patriots had never forgotten that Silesia was a lost parcel of property which their forefathers had been unable to retain against the wishes of the Habsburg dynasty.[1] Hardly had the old chancellor von Ludewig in Halle received notification of the Emperor's death than he informed the young King in Rheinsberg[2] that for forty years he had been gathering evidence to support Prussia's claims to Silesia. He cited as the person originally responsible for his efforts the late minister von Ilgen, adviser

[1] Silesia, often referred to as a duchy, was subdivided in medieval times into a number of individual duchies and other lesser-ranking territorial units. All of them came under Habsburg jurisdiction through Austria's acquisition of the Bohemian Crown (1526), which held the right of suzerainty. However, already in 1523 the collateral Hohenzollern line of Brandenburg-Ansbach had purchased the Principality of Jägerndorf (plus Oderberg and Beuthen) from the local ruler. Austria confiscated the area at the outset of the Thirty Years' War because the Margrave was a partisan of the Protestant cause in Bohemia (Ban of the Empire, 1621). The main Hohenzollern line had also concluded an inheritance treaty (1507) with the indigenous Piast family that governed in Brieg, Liegnitz, and Wohlau.

When this dynasty died out in 1675, the Habsburgs forced the Great Elector to give up his claims in return for the little district of Schwiebus, a part of the Principality of Glogau. The weak King Frederick I returned Schwiebus to Austria but not without disavowing his father's formal renunciation. Thus Koser's assertion is a nationalistically tinged overstatement.—Ed.

[2] Rheinsberg was a lovely, baroque country villa north of Berlin to which the tyrannical Frederick William I permitted his browbeaten son to retire in 1736.—Ed.

*From Reinhold Koser, *Geschichte Friedrichs des Grossen*, vol. 1 (Stuttgart: J. G. Cotta'sche Buchhandlung Nachfolger, 1912), pp. 235–241. Translated by Thomas M. Barker.

to three rulers, whom a grateful King Frederick William I had called "a good, faithful, old Brandenburg patriarch." Ilgen, so Ludewig, added, had been of the opinion that with the extinction of the Habsburg male line these claims would sooner or later be raised.

On the same November 1 that Ludewig was writing from Halle, Treasury President von Rochow, resident in Cleves, called Frederick's attention to an old draft plan of the Great Elector for acquiring Silesia, the original of which had been discovered inside a long-forgotten secretary on the royal estate of Ruheleben near Spandau. This find was worth more to him than a gift of 10,000 ducats, Frederick William I had said at the time. Rochow now regarded it as his duty to refer the son to the words of the father and the plans of the greatgrandfather. Frederick answered with thanks, mentioning that he was already acquainted with the manuscript. His father had probably given it to him, and if the project had been in the making for some time, then the memory of the Great Elector's draft had its share in the decision.

In short, the admonitions of the two faithful, old state servants were unnecessary. Immediately upon receipt of the news from Vienna the King commanded one of his ministers and one of his generals, namely, Podewils and Schwerin, to come to Rheinsberg to take part in a crown council of the most memorable nature.

The highly educated, cosmopolitan Kurt Christoph von Schwerin, well-tested both as a soldier and as a diplomat, had been personally close to his master for a long time. He had been promoted to the rank of field marshal and raised to the dignity of count shortly after Frederick's accession to the throne. The cabinet minister Podewils, solely responsible for the foreign ministry since the death of Thule-

meister, had not yet enjoyed a position of confidence.

Heinrich von Podewils, then sixty-four, combined impeccable fidelity to duty, indefatigable energy, the ability to make acute judgments of persons and situations, a very exact knowledge of the diplomatic terrain, and broad skill in the art of negotiation with a reluctance to make fundamental decisions and to enter upon new and uncharted courses of action. He manifested a caution and anxiety which his present sovereign regarded as the hereditary failing of Prussian statesmen from the school of the old von Ilgen. . . . At the moment Podewils' greatest worry was that the new monarch would not want to decide in favor of a strong alliance or choose a hard and fast political system. . . . Since the Emperor's death seemed to heighten European international difficulties at a time already sufficiently troubled, Podewils composed another of his memoranda. He sought to illuminate all aspects of the world situation now altered by the great event in Vienna and to indicate the presumptive advantages of this state of affairs for the objectives of Prussian foreign policy as he understood it.

In all likelihood he had scarcely laid down his pen when the King's order called him to Rheinsberg. There he now learned that Frederick intended to drop the hereditary claims to Berg [the main part of the later Ruhr] in favor of Silesia and to utilize them only as bargaining points. An objective that the minister had for years considered as valuable as it would be difficult to attain now seemed hardly worth the effort of a *coup de main* in comparison with the exalted goal Frederick had set.

The decision was hard and fast. Podewils and Schwerin were called upon for advice only on ways and means of executing it. They spent three days in Rheins-berg. The discussion was so lively that the King, contrary to his habit, failed to dine at the Queen's table. On the second day (October 29) the two royal confidants summarized in a memorandum the substance of the consultations insofar as the political aspects of the question were concerned. With more refined diplomatic slyness than protocollary exactitude, Podewils gave the document a form in which, quite obviously, the real opinion of the King was not clearly expressed.

The memorandum states that there were two possibilities: Frederick's acquisition of Silesia through negotiations with the Viennese Court, using the maritime powers as mediators; or by military conquest in association with France and its friends.

The first approach appeared safest to the two authors and least subject to chance. In its distress the Viennese Court might open negotiations on its own, might make offers. But should it hesitate, and in order to gain time, let Prussia break the ice. Let one offer to defend the Austrian hereditary lands, let one promise Brandenburg's imperial electoral vote for the spouse of Charles VI's female heir [Francis of Lorraine] and renunciation of the Jülich-Berg claims, to which Austria had been so opposed in the past. Finally, hint about the prospect of a few million talers from the Prussian treasury. If negotiations in Vienna were successful, the Austro-Prussian alliance could be strengthened by inviting the maritime powers and Russia to participate. If the negotiations met with difficulty, one could request these powers to intervene, always realizing that French predominance had to be resisted, as in the era of Louis XIV.

If all these efforts to win over the Viennese Court by direct negotiations or through foreign mediators proved in vain, there was the second, opposite approach. One would place one's self on the side of France. One would also conclude a partition agreement with the courts of Munich and Dresden, recognizing their claims to the Austrian inheritance. Lastly, one would support the candidacy of the Elector of Bavaria for the imperial crown. Of course it would be imperative to have protection from possible Russian attack; this could be accomplished by means of alliances or diversionary actions. For help in conquering Silesia, the prospective allies would be rewarded with Jülich and Berg.

"These are," the memorandum continued, "the only two plans Your Majesty gave us the honor to discuss yesterday, but we did then speak of a third."

Should Saxony bestir itself and assault Bohemia or Silesia, the King would then be justified, according to Podewils and Schwerin, if he followed its example with respect to Silesia. For he would have to prevent himself from being completely surrounded and the opening of a theater of war on his borders. With a pawn in his hands, he would have the advantage of being able to initiate negotiations concerning cession with much greater chances of success.

Although the memorandum is silent about the matter, in the oral deliberations the King unquestionably regarded as essential that which Podewils and Schwerin considered advisable only under certain conditions: that is, seizure of Silesia not *after* but *before* negotiations. Only in this way does the reference at the end of the document — the possibility of force — make any sense. Despite its outward form the suggestion for prior seizure did not originate with the two advisers. In view of their overall pacific stance this could hardly have been possible. The addendum was, rather, an attempt to delimit the plan for attack by establishing prerequisites for a given instance. Furthermore, only in this fashion can one explain the written exchange of arguments and counterarguments that took place between the King and Podewils after the latter's return to Berlin. In this correspondence the question was narrowed down to the point of asking which of the three formally discussed courses of action the King should accept, or simply whether he ought to go his own way, that is, aim for Silesia forthwith.

"I am going to give you a problem to solve," Frederick wrote to his minister on November 1. "If one has an advantage, shouldn't one exploit it? I am prepared with my troops and with everything else. If I do not make use of my resources, then I am keeping in my hands a possession the purpose of which I fail to recognize. If I make use of it, people will say that I am clever enough to avail myself of the superiority which I enjoy over my neighbors."

As Frederick wrote these lines, it was as if he knew how his father had been spoken of in Vienna. "The King of Prussia will not have his army march, for he is a poltroon." These were the words with which Count Sinzendorf, the Court Chancellor, once let someone console him when he became worried about Prussia. It was on this basis that Austrian policy toward Frederick William I had always proceeded.

Upon receipt of the royal missive of November 1, Podewils wrote to Schwerin that the fever was mounting rather than dropping and that in view of the ineffectiveness of their representations they would have no choice other than the glory of obedience.

Podewils made one last effort to sway

his master by bringing the principle of experience to bear upon the royal "problem": even when one seems to possess great superiority, fortune has all too often deserted a martial enterprise. The other side of the coin frequently has a different face. Podewils reminded the King of Charles Gustaf of Sweden who had conquered all of Poland and then lost it, of Louis XIV who fared no differently after the rapid occupation of Holland. Thus, before entering a war, the strongest party does well—as France did in 1733[3]—to assure itself of an ally on whom it can fall back if necessary. And Prussia is not a neatly rounded-off and strictly unitary state like France. Rather, the scattered nature of its possessions deprives its armed forces of cohesion. The rear, the flanks, and the heart of the country are open to any attack whatsoever in more than one place.

Frederick was fully aware of his responsibility in making this decision. He wrote at the time quite earnestly, "For a week great events have been succeeding each other one right after the other, and so politics have reached a peak of intensity. Matters are beginning to take such a serious course that it requires more than customary wisdom to find one's way. In order to do the right thing one would need to peer into the future and be able to read in the book of fate about the conjunctures and combinations of future times."

On November 6, after he had worked out a detailed argumentation, he sent Podewils his "Ideas Concerning Political Projects Being Drafted on the Occasion of the Emperor's Death" and asked him to express his objections with all possible

---

[3] The reference is to the War of the Polish Succession, in which France was able to acquire Lorraine.—Ed.

candor. In opposition to the doctrine that no war may be commenced without allies, the King held to his thesis that complete readiness to strike was unquestionably Prussia's main advantage and strength, momentarily providing unlimited superiority over all other European powers. To wait until Saxony and Bavaria set the example with an attack of their own meant permitting the Saxon neighbor to aggrandize himself in complete contravention of Prussia's interest. The minister asked for allies. The King replied with the clear, simple, and basic consideration upon which all his political calculations since his accession had rested: "England and France are at odds. If France meddles in German affairs, England cannot stand by idly; hence one of the two opposing parties will always be able to offer me a good alliance. If one does not reap advantage with England and Holland, one will surely be able to do so with France."

Thus these two great powers canceled each other out. Russia, however, required a particular counterbalance. The King's "Ideas" proceeded to point out that there were all kinds of resources for this purpose, in the worst instance simply a declaration of war by Sweden. And should the sick Empress Anna happen to pass away, Russia would be more than occupied on the domestic front.

From his whole argumentation the King concluded that "one must gain possession of Silesia before winter and negotiate during the winter. One will then always be able to choose sides. Already in possession of the territory, we can bargain successfully, whereas any other procedure would deprive us of our advantage. We will never get anything at all merely by negotiating, or else burdensome conditions will be imposed upon us in return for granting us mere trifles."

Podewils received the "Ideas" on the same evening. He spent the night in putting to paper the objections the King had requested. As the news had just arrived that the Elector of Bavaria had announced his claims to the Austrian succession in Vienna and since the Saxon resident [chargé d'affaires] had already informed Podewils that the king of Poland [simultaneously Elector of Saxony] would be inclined to follow an example set by Bavaria, the precondition that Podewils and Schwerin had sought to attach to Prussia's raising of arms during the Rheinsberg meeting was now fulfilled, at least to a degree. And so Podewils visibly began to beat a retreat. He warned once more of sacrificing the certain acquistion of the Duchy of Berg to the uncertain gain of Silesia. He once again exhausted all possibilities: that by sacrificing the Austrian Netherlands the Viennese Court might throw itself into the arms of the French or buy itself the support of the Elector of Bavaria; or that the Saxons and the Hannoverians might join Austria against Prussia because of border jealousies, reinforced by troops of the Estates of the Empire and by the Danes; that Russia might send 30,000 men for the allied Viennese Court; or that the Poles might fall upon the New March—all of these were objections which the King had already rejected as unsound and to which he now once again opposed his favorite dictum, namely that England would always defend whoever was attacked by France and vice versa. When, to culminate matters, the news arrived that even the King of Sardinia was rousing himself and arming, the King in his answer to Podewils (November 7) ended the debate, begun on October 28, with the announcement that he had despatched mobilization orders to his regiments the same day.

On November 9 he received news of the long-expected demise of the Tsarina, who had succumbed to her painful ailments only eight days after Charles' death. The one loophole in his political scheme was now plugged. "God favors us, and good fortune is on our side," he wrote to Podewils.

The die was cast. . . .

HEINRICH RITTER VON SRBIK (1878–1951) was
associated with the University of Vienna from 1922
to 1945. As the standard-bearer of Pan-German
historiography within the Habsburg monarchy, he
had many gifted disciples such as Reinhold Lorenz
and Hugo Hantsch, who later became champion of
the Austro-Catholic school of thought. Srbik was
president of the Viennese section of the Academy
of Sciences during the *Anschluss* and was forced
to retire at the end of the war along with other
compromised academic figures. His works include
studies of German humanism, Wallenstein, and
Metternich and a post-1945 reevaluation of Austria's
historical mission. His great classic on German unity,
from which the following selection is taken, presents
a destructive Frederick and the fateful Silesian
struggle as one feature of the background to the great
political issues of the succeeding century.*

Heinrich Ritter von Srbik

Berlin and Vienna: Tragic Antipodes

The Emperor and the Hohenzollern
Elector fought together more than once
against the Swedes, the French, and the
Turks during the seventeenth century.
More than once they did battle side by
side during the worldwide conflict over the
Spanish inheritance. But the concept
of *Kaiser* and *Reich*, a Catholic disposition
and Austrian *raison d'état,* universalist
traditions, rational self-interest politics,
and vital instincts, caused the Habsburg
rulers Leopold I, Joseph I, and Charles
VI to throw obstacles in the path of an
awakening and power-hungry Electorate
of Brandenburg and to make concessions
only involuntarily, whether it was a
matter of Swedish possessions on imperial
soil [Swedish Pomerania, Rügen, Wismar,
and Bremen-Verden] or the territories
of the lower Rhine [Jülich, Berg, Cleves,
Mark, and Ravensberg]. In Prussia it
was held that the opposition of the Habsburgs to the rise of Brandenburg could
be traced back to the time of Emperor
Ferdinand II. In any event the policy of
the Habsburgs was guided by the sure
knowledge that a rival to the Empire
and their own dynastic state was arising
in the northeastern part of Germany—a
competitor whose vital law was opposition
to the *status quo,* who represented movement in the face of inertia. Again and
again there were sharp conflicts which
reflected the contrast between the impe-

---

*From Heinrich Ritter von Srbik, *Deutsche Einheit,* vol. 1, 3d ed. (Munich: F. Bruckmann, KG, 1935),
pp. 97–103. Translated by Thomas M. Barker. Numerous footnotes omitted.

rial-Habsburg consciousness of sovereignty and the Hohenzollern sense of
stately identity, the latter a force hostile
to Austria's hegemony in the Empire
and its great-power status in southeastern
Central Europe. Ultimately King Frederick William I even sought to use the
[collateral] Franconian margraviates of
Ansbach and Bayreuth as outposts and
props for Prussian power in southern
Germany. These principalities, which
became flourishing cultural centers, also
evolved into an object of rivalry both in
Habsburg-Hohenzollern sphere-of-influ-
ence politics and in imperial tradition
and the more specific Prussian drive for
power. The twin states remained an object
of strife for the two great adversaries
Maria Theresa and Frederick, until they
finally fell under permanent Prussian
control in 1791.

Frederick II was the great wrecker of
the Empire and of its Habsburg-Austrian
headship. "The *sacra maiestas* and imperial authority," it has been said quite
correctly, "seemed to him a highly pro-
fane thing, an old inventory item and
trusty tool of Austrian policy."[1] Frederick
put an end to the condition of tension
between the imperial princely and European status of his country, a phenomenon
that had still crippled the energies of
his father.

The future king grew up in a lonely
fashion, a stranger to his father and the
latter's stultifying drill because of his
own highly delicate and sensitive nature,
a dreamer without any impulse for work,
stuffed full of idealistic political views
without any real schooling in politics,
and inclined to a theoretical, historical
version of political science. Thirsting for

freedom, lacking any firm religious faith,
and with a strong bent for literature and
science, not at all soldierly, forced to
engage in practical service to the state,[2]
Frederick cherished even during his
youth no deep feeling of community with
Emperor and Empire. The youthful
Crown Prince—whose position *vis-à-vis*
the mistrusting and cruelly harsh King
Frederick William, Charles VI sustained by providing, *inter alia*, an annual
pension—experienced no feelings of
gratitude toward the Habsburg, the go-
between in arranging his loveless mar-
riage. For Frederick, who already in
1731 was weighing the expansion of
Prussia to include Swedish Pomerania,
Mecklenburg, Jülich, and Berg, the idea
of a marital link with Charles' daughter
had only the value of gaining as a dowry
a few duchies in Silesia. To him, Austria
was only one great power among others.
Participation in Eugene of Savoy's Rhenine campaign (1735) only increased his
alienation from the Empire. He became
a "secret partisan of the French cause."
Indeed, love of glory and striving for
power, incongruously paired with the
philosophic impulse for justice, had led
him to advocate privately a French alliance already in 1734. During the Rheinsberg period of reading and reflection
—when the desire to conquer receded and
political morality seemed to be winning
out—he was embittered against the Empire and Austria because of the Emperor's
failure to keep a pledge to help Prussia
acquire Berg. His French inclinations
were solidly reinforced when he observed
his father's inability to achieve great
deeds. The defeats of the Imperial Army
in the Turkish War [1737–1739] appeared
to him as punitive acts of God. In his

---

[1] Reinhold Koser, "Brandenburg-Preussen im
Kampf zwischen Imperialismus und Libertät,"
Historische Zeitschrift, XCVI (1875), 222.

[2] Frederick was compelled to work as an administrative apprentice for some time.—Ed.

"Considérations sur l'état présent du corps politique d'Europe" Frederick, always much more a theoretician, more a political idealist inspired by literary and philosophical ambition, than a realist, opposed to the "despotism" of Austria the concept of imperial law, an approach entirely within the framework of the old "liberties" of the Imperial Estates. When the author of *The Antimachiavell*, a book pregnant with the elementary will to rule, became king, his hatred for the Empire and his rejection of Prussian subservience to Vienna caused him to label the office of emperor "the phantom of an ideal which once possessed strength" but which "nowadays means nothing at all."

The death of Charles VI was a "bagatelle" to him. He quickly threw over the rudder of his ship of state. It was not Berg that became his destination but rather Silesia. The imperial question *per se* was irrelevant to him. Ambition, yearning for glory, sober and elementary power politics dominated his actions. Without a moment's hesitation and thinking only of the interest of Prussia he supported the imperial candidacy of Charles VII, which favored Bavarian and French goals in Germany. To the King only the Brandenburg-Prussian monarchy was "a concrete, guiding, supreme moral instance." Likewise, in legal form, the Roman Emperor should be equal to, not higher than the King of Prussia. "Authority" in the French-Bavarian-Prussian system should reside with Prussia and the "burden" with Bavaria. In 1744 Frederick forestalled the Empire's recovery of Alsace. He sought to bring about a "union" of Imperial Estates under Prussian leadership in order to further the cause of the Wittelsbach Emperor and of Prussian power with the aid of the imperial constitution. His project failed on this occasion, but despite its defeat imperial plans

remained a leitmotiv in the future course of his life. He strove to secure a financial basis of power for the Bavarian emperor by proposing secularization of the south German ecclesiastical principalities in the same way that a league of Imperial Circuits[3] was intended to provide a military foundation. However, the King of Prussia was supposed to receive the title of "Permanent Lieutenant General"[4] and supreme command over the Imperial Army. The Bavarian imperial incumbency was for him only an instrument in the struggle against the Habsburgs and a means for achieving a hegemony of Prussian military power in Germany. This policy, too, was a Friderican legacy. When Prussia's objectives in the Empire were frustrated with the accession to office of the Lorrainer Francis I, Frederick was once again compelled to think in terms of a "phantom." Austrian imperial authority remained the enemy of his royal existence. It is a matter of the greatest symbolic significance that in 1750 he forbade intercessory prayers for the Emperor in his lands as an "ancient, malevolently invented custom." For a king of Prussia the acquisition of a province was more worthwhile than the "empty title" of Emperor. How could the great imperial trial which was to have been conducted against him for having disturbed the peace of the land still have been carried out, and how could "Frederick the Great, fulfilling his duty as Imperial Archchamberlain, have extended a silver handwashing basin to Joseph II at the latter's coronation banquet in 1764"?

---

[3] The Circuit, a constitutional relic dating from the period 1500–1512, was a shadowy organization comprising the territorial states within a given geographic region.—Ed.

[4] In the seventeenth and eighteenth centuries this was the highest possible military rank, to which even that of field marshal was subordinate.—Ed.

Did the ideas of the old Ascanian dynasty[5] influence his thoughts in a way that even he did not realize? His clearly perceptible, geographic goal was to seize the glacis of Fortress Bohemia from the Habsburgs or to remove it from their grasp if he could not succeed in smashing the position. He conquered the Silesian glacis. At the height of his victories in 1758–1759 he was aiming for the Saxon glacis as well as for Mecklenburg. However, this hotly desired prize was denied him. Frederick did not want the permanent destruction of Austria. If Spanish and French plans to partition the Habsburg inheritance with the help of Prussia had come about, the Southern Netherlands and the Italian outposts of the Empire would have fallen into the hands of the Latin states. Bohemia would have formed the main basis of the Bavarian *Imperium* just as Silesia had become the underpinning of Hohenzollern great-power status. A divided German center would have become the plaything of France.

As a result of the expulsion of the Habsburgs, Silesia was lost to the Holy Roman Empire not *de jure* but *de facto*. The conqueror regarded his newly gained territory as withdrawn from the Empire, as a fully sovereign duchy like the Duchy of Prussia [later East Prussia]. By excluding Silesia in order to magnify the overall European great-power status of his kingdom, he narrowed the confines of the Empire. Already at the time of the Kleinschnellendorf Convention [October 9, 1741] he had wished to acquire the Duchy of Lower Silesia and have the County of Glatz released not only from the tie of fealty of Bohemia but free of subjection to the imperial law of fealty. He actually

succeeded in obtaining cession in "full sovereignty and independence" of the Crown of Bohemia through the Preliminary Peace of Breslau (Wroclaw) [June 6, 1742]. In 1751 the Empire assumed the role of guarantor of the Peace of Dresden [December 25, 1745], which confirmed that of Breslau.[6] It was believed that Prussian Silesia[7] had left the framework of the Empire *de facto* in 1742 and also *de jure* in 1751. This assumption was purportedly buttressed by the fact that the Emperor neglected to list the Duchies of Silesia and Prussia by name in the *privilegium de non appellando* [immunity from appellate jurisdiction] which he granted the Kingdom of Prussia. However, legally speaking, even after its cession by Maria Theresa, Silesia remained a constituent part of the Empire, which provided its 1741 guarantee only with the proviso of retaining the *iurium imperii* [imperial law]. The Empire never renounced the nexus of fealty; the Queen of Bohemia [Maria Theresa's only imperial title at the time] would never have been able to confer full sovereignty upon indirect fiefs of the Empire. Thus an unclear constitutional relationship was created, analogous to the fiction of the Republic of the United Netherlands belonging to the Empire long after the former had become an autonomous power separate from Spain, a situation comparable to the obscure and contradictory clauses of the Peace of Westphalia regarding Alsace. But, of course, what did a

---

[5] The reference is to the family that ruled Brandenburg during the Central Middle Ages.—Ed.

[6] The Preliminary Peace was *initially* confirmed at Berlin on July 28, 1742, but Frederick, afraid that Austria was making too great progress against its other enemies in the Succession struggle, reentered the conflict in 1744. Having inflicted serious defeats upon the Habsburg army, he once again deserted his allies, hence the Peace of Dresden.—Ed.

[7] A section of Silesia remained Austrian (parts of Neisse, Jägerndorf, Troppau (Opava), and all of Teschen (Tešin).—Ed.

reservation of imperial rights over Silesia actually mean to a monarch in whose mind the Empire should be a republic of princes which at some future point would dissolve into independent states? Samuel von Cocceji's reform of justice did away with the last connection between Prussia and the imperial court system. And what hardfisted grandeur of destruction and rebuilding lay in the plan Frederick pursued in the fall of 1759; namely, to divide northern Germany between Hannover and Prussia, which "should tear themselves loose from the Holy Roman Empire and establish independent realms by themselves"?

For Austria the loss of Silesia meant not only the illegal seizure of a gleaming jewel from the Habsburg diadem of kingdoms and provinces; not only the loss of a priceless "fabricant and forwarding agent" in the economic life of the monarchy; not only a weakening in human terms of some 1,200,000 persons. The cession also most severely damaged the imperial foundations of the Central European colonial power structure of the Habsburgs, already shaken when the Lausitz was turned over to Saxony [1635]. It delivered the lands of the Bohemian Crown, the link between the German northeast and southeast, to a prospective Slavic majority. It released Austria from its ancient and esteemed duty of functioning as the Empire's first bulwark against France insofar as the Habsburg position of imperial leadership was destroyed. It robbed the Habsburgs of the region from which they had been able to reach into northeastern Germany. The loss of the province further deprived them of a favorable strategic stance *vis-à-vis* Polish and Hungarian territory. It drove Austria all the more toward a Danubian state existence, and by diminishing the German land surface of the archhouse it made

the latter's southeastern German cultural mission more difficult. Paired with the dualism of power politics in the living space of the Germans—amid which the atomized old Germany could hardly count as a unit—was an intellectual dichotomy, in which a single personality stepped alongside the old ideal of a German emperor-state. For that which most impressed large numbers of the German people was the fact that an individual fought on to final victory with almost inconceivable spiritual strength after seven years of gigantic struggle against the other great powers; that a German prince could beat the French; that a German prince sealed off the northeastern Central European region by acquiring West Prussia [Pomerelia], in the same way that Austria was seeking to seal off the southeast, for the good of Germandom and associate peoples; that a German prince became the founder of a state through even greater self-abnegation, through devotion of his whole person to the cause of the country, and with a most profound, if nonreligious feeling of responsibility.

And this prince was not the Emperor, who was after all descended from the non-German House of Lorraine, a foreign twig grafted onto the old imperial family and bearer of the imperial crown only by virtue of his Habsburg wife. The prince, who for many Germans became the incorporation of German honor and the typical German hero, was the greatest enemy of Holy Roman power. He was perfector of a state entity that reached out beyond the Habsburgs, the Wettiners, and the Guelphs and creator of Prussian national and state sentiment. German pride in the great Frederick had no particularly Prussian content outside of Prussia. It was German will power and the deeds of a born leader. It was masculinity and the heroic quality, the willingness to sacrifice one's self for the good of the fatherland, the talent to build and to educate people to a concept of statehood even if still German-territorial. Therein lay the magic that caused so many Germans to overlook the breach with the ancient, universalistic German ideal and the immeasurable damage to a southeastern Germandom, heavily engaged in a struggle to retain control of its geographic space. It was a charm which, paradoxically, filled non-Prussian Germans with admiration for a champion who was himself anything but national-minded. One may ask whether German values were not actually present in the strengthening of German self-awareness, in the new impulses favoring German state consciousness, in uttermost, duty-bound labor for the state. But one is tempted to reply that the price of these gains was very high.

G. P. GOOCH (1874–1968) is remembered by those who knew him personally as a kindly, gracious person. A child prodigy, he joined the Liberal party at an early age and entered upon a brief Parliamentary career. Later he became editor of the prestigious *Contemporary Review*. Trained in the sparkling environment of turn-of-the-century Cambridge, he was an insatiable reader, and his published works include more than a dozen delightfully written volumes, especially on the eighteenth and nineteenth century. Historiography was his particular interest and forte. His activities in other areas of intellectual and public endeavor were legion. The student may ask whether the sharp reprimand he accorded Frederick does Gooch, the man, greater or lesser credit.*

G. P. Gooch

A Great Historical Crime

If anything was more repulsive than the decision to steal a portion of his neighbour's vineyard it was the attempt to dress up the crime as a service to the prospective victim. "The House of Austria," explained Frederick to his uncle George II, "exposed to all its enemies since the loss of its head and the total disintegration of its affairs, is on the point of succumbing under the efforts of those who openly advance claims to the succession and secretly plan to seize a part. And as owing to the situation of my territories I have the chief interest in averting the consequences and above all in preventing those who may have formed the design to seize Silesia, the bulwark of my possessions, I have been compelled to send my troops into the Duchy in order to prevent others seizing it, to my great disadvantage and to the prejudice of the just claims which my House has always had to the larger part of that country. I have no other purpose than the preservation and the real benefit of the House of Austria." Before giving the signal which for a generation was to drench Europe with blood, the aggressor despatched his terms to Vienna to be presented directly the Silesian frontier was crossed. He had recognised the succession of Maria Theresa and written her friendly letters. Now he would guarantee all possessions of the House of Austria in Germany, form a close alliance with the Court of Vienna, Russia and the Maritime

*From G. P. Gooch, *Frederick the Great: the Ruler, the Writer, the Man* (London: Longmans, Green & Company Ltd., 1947), pp. 8–12.

Powers, use all his influence to procure the election of her husband the Duke of Lorraine as Emperor, and supply two or even three million florins. Such valuable services and the risks they entailed would require a proportionate reward, namely the cession of the whole of Silesia. It was in vain that the friendly British Government advised Vienna's acceptance of these terms. Though he pretended to be surprised and shocked by Maria Theresa's indignant reaction to the attempted blackmail, Frederick would have despised her had she submitted, and she alone of the crowned heads of Europe won his abiding respect. . . .

Neither Frederick nor Podewils nor the jurists, however, suggested that Prussia had a legal right to the whole of Silesia: the claim was only to the four duchies of Liegnitz, Brieg, Wohlau and Jägerndorf. Carlyle's characterisation of the rape as "a rushing out to seize your own stolen horse" is grotesque, but Vienna had had plenty of warnings that the claims of the House of Brandenburg would one day be revived.

These arguments were mainly for the Chancelleries, the public and posterity. The King would probably have seized the coveted province had there been no claims at all, as he almost admitted in the celebrated letter to Jordan of March 3, 1741. "My youth, the fire of passions, the desire for glory, yes, to be frank, even curiosity, finally a secret instinct, has torn me away from the delights of tranquillity. The satisfaction of seeing my name in the papers and later in history has seduced me." Yet this damaging confession must not be taken as a complete explanation of the step which opened a new chapter of European history as surely as the cannonade at Valmy half a century later. The deeper cause was the resolve to secure for Prussia the status of a Great Power, to grasp the rich prize to which he thought her entitled by her vital needs and growing strength. In his own striking phrase she was a hermaphrodite, more Electorate than Kingdom. His dominions were scattered across northern Europe from the Rhineland to the Russian frontier, the central core being separated from the outlying possessions by blocks of foreign territory. Cleve, Mark and Ravensberg could not be defended against France, nor East Prussia against Russia, and the frontier of Saxony was only thirty miles from Berlin. His most plausible argument was found in the map of his heritage, a thing of shreds and patches unique in Germany. Such sprawling possessions clamoured for a change, and Silesia was the first and most important item in the programme of consolidation. A further consideration was the extreme poverty of his inheritance, much of it consisting of sand and forest. Even his father's energy could never extract from the little state the resources needed to secure and maintain a place in the sun. More taxpayers, more soldiers, more food, more industries were urgently required. The patriotic purpose was assumed to justify the means. "Frederick the Great stole Silesia," remarked Bismarck to the elder Bülow, "yet he is one of the greatest men of all time."

When every allowance has been made for ancient claims and for the fact that moral considerations meant little to any eighteenth-century ruler except Maria Theresa, the rape of Silesia ranks with the partition of Poland among the sensational crimes of modern history. Austria was taken completely by surprise. Though Macaulay's essay on Frederick the Great is among his weakest performances, his rhetoric contains a good deal of truth. The Pragmatic Sanction, he declares, was placed under the protection of the public faith of the whole civilised world. "Even if no positive stipulations had existed, the arrangement was one which no good man would have been willing to disturb. It was an arrangement acceptable to the great population whose happiness was chiefly concerned. It was an arrangement which made no change in the distribution of power among the states of Christendom. It was an arrangement which could be set aside only by means of a general war. The sovereigns of Europe were therefore bound by every obligation which those who are entrusted with power over their fellow-creatures ought to hold most sacred to respect and defend the rights of the Archduchess. Her situation and her personal qualities were such as might be expected to move the mind of any generous man to pity, admiration and chivalrous tenderness. But the selfish rapacity of the King of Prussia gave the signal to his neighbours. The whole world sprang to arms. On the head of Frederick is all the blood which was shed in every quarter of the globe. The evils produced by his wickedness were felt in lands where the name of Prussia was unknown, and in order that he might rob a neighbour whom he had promised to defend, black men fought on the coast of Coromandel and red men scalped each other by the Great Lakes of North America."

That the aggressor had promised to defend Maria Theresa is untrue: his father had accepted the Pragmatic Sanction, but he never undertook to fight for it. Here is Frederick's reply to this particular charge, extracted from the Memorandum drafted in his own hand and, after revision by Podewils, circulated to his representatives at foreign Courts. "It would be wrong to accuse the King of infringing the Pragmatic Sanction. His Majesty does not contest the succession in Austria but is merely maintaining his own rights of which the late Emperor could not dispose since they were not his property and which for that reason he could not transmit to his daughter. Moreover, the House of Austria could not demand the fulfillment of the guarantee promised by the late King of Prussia in a treaty between that prince and the Emperor Charles VI, since that monarch, far from carrying out its obligations, made another contract diametrically opposed to it in a manner which reflects little honour on the good faith of the Court of Vienna." If the young King had contented himself with the four duchies to which alone he laid claim, his reasoning would have been more impressive; but since even such a limited demand would undoubtedly have been refused he threw legality to the winds and gambled for the larger prize.

OTTO HINTZE (1861–1941), born at Pyritz (Pyrzyce) in Pomerania, became a student of the nationalistic Droysen and ultimately held a professorship at the University of Berlin (1913–1923). First interested in the development of Brandenburg-Prussia, he later devoted himself to comparative constitutional and administrative history. His specialized studies continue to have great value. The following selection from his survey account of the Hohenzollern dynasty shows even greater pride in Prussian accomplishments than is the case with Koser. Hintze tells us not only that Frederick was a consummate diplomat but also that his actions resulted in great material blessings.*

Otto Hintze

Masterly Diplomacy: A Beneficial New Order

In the period after the Seven Years' War, as far as foreign policy was concerned, Frederick relied mainly upon an alliance with Russia, concluded April 11, 1764. He always considered this agreement to have the greatest possible value as it enabled him to avoid the danger of complete isolation in international affairs. The Polish question, which became an object of concern on the death of Augustus III (October 5, 1763), provided the bridge for an understanding between Prussia and Russia. Already then the basic issue was which of the big European states would gain control, in one form or another, of this completely decrepit kingdom. In keeping with age-old tradition, every new royal election turned into a free-for-all as the ambitions of the major Continental powers collided. Since the War of the [Polish] Succession of 1733, which had placed Augustus III on his throne, Russian influence had prevailed, and this posed a grave threat to Prussia. During the Seven Years' War Poland remained nominally neutral, but in reality it became the operational basis for Russian armies, and on several occasions Polish volunteer corps served Austria and Russia in their common struggle against Prussia. The Russo-Austrian system, upon which the Polish kingship of the Saxon-born Augustus depended, broke down after the Seven Years' War.

*With kind permission of Verlag Paul Parey, Hamburg and Berlin, taken from their publication *Die Hohenzollern und ihr Werk* by Otto Hintze (Berlin 1915), pp. 389–390. Translated by Thomas M. Barker.

With the Peace of Hubertusburg, Austria once more tied its fortunes more closely to France. France, on the other hand, was most strongly opposed to Russian rule in Poland, the obvious goal of Catherine the Great. Austria thus found itself in opposition to Russia, the consequence of which was to drive Russia in the direction of Prussia.

Frederick was by no means blind to the ambitious objectives of Russian foreign policy. He foresaw that if they were ever realized Russia would be able to terrorize all Europe. But, as he himself stated, in order to gain a few years of secure peace (required for purposes of domestic reconstruction), he was compelled to seize upon the Russian alliance and thus also to support Catherine's foreign policy objectives, at least partially.

Both sides agreed in advance that no Austrian candidate—and certainly not another Saxon prince—would be permitted to acquire the Polish crown. They had no difficulty in settling upon the person whom the Poles were to choose. Catherine suggested her exlover, the Polish nobleman Stanisław Poniatowki, who was sure of the support of a powerful indigenous faction since he was the nephew of Prince Czartoryski . . . It was also agreed that the Polish constitution with its elective kingship and the *liberum veto*—that is, anarchy and impotence—should be preserved and that protection of the Dissidents, especially the millions of adherents of the Orthodox Church (deprived by the Jesuit Counter Reformation of both political and civil rights), should devolve jointly upon the two powers. Russia, however, was far more concerned with this issue than Prussia.

This, then, was the basis for Frederick's defensive pact with Russia, initially concluded for eight years and later renewed with the provision that if either party should be attacked the other would come to its aid with a contingent of 12,000 troops or with equivalent subsidies. Thereupon it also became possible to proceed with the election (September 7) of King Stanis-ławski, naturally under Russian pressure but without any opposition on the part of the great powers.

Catherine now began to exercise vigorously her right to protect Orthodox fellow believers in Poland and thus gradually to bring the country under her full control. This development held great peril for Frederick. Yet even in Poland Catherine's plans met resistance. The result was a civil war, in which Russian troops intervened. The Turkish border was violated in the process, and this led to a simultaneous war between the Ottoman Empire and Russia. Frederick now faced the unpleasant necessity of paying subsidies to St. Petersburg in fulfillment of his treaty obligation. Russia's successes in the Turkish war and its intention of keeping Moldavia and Wallachia (which it had occupied) aroused the greatest concern in Austria. The Habsburgs were not prepared to tolerate such a tightening of Russian pressure on their borders. There was acute danger of war between Austria and Russia. If, as was to be expected, Russia were the party attacked, then its ally, Frederick, would have to participate in a conflict entirely foreign to his interests.

In order to counter this peril the King tried to mediate a Russo-Turkish peace agreement that would dispel the worries of the Austrians and hence the risk of war. But persuading the Russians to give up the Danubian principalities proved to be extraordinarily difficult. The only possibility was to find a substitute for those provinces by partitioning Polish territory. Frederick, who had been eyeing West Prussia[1] ever since his youth, had suggested the idea already once at the very beginning of the whole affair. But a cautiously unveiled hint of Prussian desires, linked to a cession of Polish lands to Russia and Austria, had been received so unfavorably at the time (1768) by the Russian minister Panin that Frederick lost all hope of realizing his project. He contented himself with renewing the

---

[1] Use of the terms "West Prussia" and "East Prussia" for prepartition times is nonhistorical. This nomenclature, which stems from postannexation administrative arrangements and which reflects modern German nationalism, has been accepted unwittingly into English usage. "Prussia," itself a word derived from the original Slavic, Borussian inhabitants of later "East" Prussia, is a Middle High German form used in the late Middle Ages as a popular synonym for the territory of the Teutonic Order. In 1525 when the Knights' lands were secularized by their Hohenzollern Grand Master, the designation "Duchy of Prussia" became official. Just a trifle smaller than within its future frontiers as "East" Prussia, it was a fief of the Polish crown, for the Order had been compelled to recognize Warsaw's suzerainty in 1460. Inherited by the main Hohenzollern line in 1618, it remained under theoretical Polish jurisdiction until 1660.

"West" Prussia's correct name for the pre-1772 period is Pomerelia. This land, originally only the eastern portion of the Piast-controlled, Elbe–Slavic-inhabited country of Pomerania, (Polish: "Pomorzhe") achieved an identity of its own about 1100 when the latter state split into two parts. The western piece, which centered on the Oder and which was subdivided several times, became an imperial fief in 1181. Thoroughly Germanized in the course of the next several centuries, "Pommern" (as its new masters called it) acquired a slice of Pomerelia in 1309 along with Brandenburg. Labeled "Polish Pomerania" or "Eastern Pomerania" by modern Polish patriots, the rest of Pomerelia simultaneously fell under the control of the Teutonic Order. However, the link to the Prussian state, fully occupied with its own colonists and the Borussi, was tenuous and relatively brief. The political concept of Pomerelia was well-enough rooted for the duchy to reemerge under the Poles in 1460. The native Kashubian people of the region even maintained a certain ethnic distinctiveness vis-à-vis both Poles and Germans until World War II. The German minority of the "Corridor," another word of later origin, was present from the thirteenth century but was not a major factor save in Danzig (Gdańsk) until Frederick's day.—Ed.

Russian alliance (October 12, 1769) so that he might be assured of Russian support in an impending controversy with the Emperor [Joseph II] over the Ansbach-Bayreuth succession. But then Austria occupied the formerly Hungarian county of Szepes (Zips, Spiš) and other adjacent Polish districts [in the Central Carpathians] as pawns in a reparations quarrel with Poland. This turn of events caused the Tsarina, in conversation with a Hohenzollern visitor, Prince Henry, to mention the possibility of Russia and Prussia also helping themselves to a piece of Poland. Of course, Catherine's idea was to toss Prussia no more than a sop, namely the Bishopric of Ermland (Warmia), a gain that Frederick would hardly find tempting by itself. On his return Prince Henry reported to the King. He depicted the mood of the Russian Court as much more positive than before, and thus it no longer seemed impossible to carry out the old plan. From that point on Frederick strove ceaselessly, and ultimately with success, to make his partition scheme the basis of an understanding between Russia and Austria and simultaneously the foundation of a Turkish peace treaty that would preserve the traditional relationship between Moldavia-Wallachia and the Porte.

The First Partition of Poland, in 1772, was a masterpiece of Friderican diplomacy. Not only was the grave danger of a major war averted, but Prussia acquired long-coveted "West" Prussia along with the Noteć (Netze) district. (Danzig-Gdańsk and Thorn-Toruń remained separate for the time being.) This territory was an ancient German colonial sphere, and now peaceful methods had restored it to rule by a German state. Since it had suffered tremendous decline while in Polish hands, it became the object of special concern on the King's part.

Whatever sort of injustice may have been committed against Poland was thus more than made up, at least before the judgment seat of an impartial brand of historiography. While for Poland it was admittedly the beginning of the end, one must emphasize strongly that the concept of the national state, dominant in European political life from the nineteenth century on had not yet been born. Likewise, nationalism had nothing to do with Frederick's motives. If the King tried, wherever possible, to substitute Germans for the inferior Polish elements of the population, he was guided more by an unconscious feeling of tribal solidarity — also deriving from the divergent levels of economic development of the two ethnic groups involved — than by any deliberate nationality principle. Such thinking was quite alien both to him and to all his contemporaries. For Frederick the main importance of this new acquisition was that it provided an indispensable link between the New March and East Prussia, thereby rounding off the eastern flank of the monarchy and making it a cohesive, at least relatively defensible region. In addition to the Warta (Warthe) and the Noteć (Netze), he now controlled a considerable stretch of the Vistula. Danzig (Gdańsk) remained part of the Polish confederation, but since both the mouth of the Vistula and Neufahrwasser (Nowy Port) had become Prussian, it was hemmed in on all sides by Prussian towns, which competed with it commercially.[2]

Clearly, the city could be regarded as a future extension, a natural culmination to the development of the already Prussian hinterland.

The King called his new possession an offshoot of anarchy. He compared it with Canada and with the Iroquois Indians. Order and a higher form of civilization became possible only with the introduction of Prussian rule. It is remarkable that this cultural activity of a Protestant state was not upset by the sectarian jealousy of the Catholic clergy. The work of colonizing West Prussia is a counterpart to Frederick William I's reestablishment of East Prussia. Roughly fifty German villages were newly founded. Polish peasants, who were serfs and whose condition was hardly distinguishable from slavery, benefitted from bestowal of the much milder status of hereditary subjection that existed in all the other Eastern provinces. On royal demesnes the peasants received hereditary proprietary rights. New settlers were admitted as legally free quitrenters. For a number of years the King granted each of the cities 100,000 talers annually to be used for rebuilding desolate sections of the city. The main difficulty was a lack of skilled workers. These were brought into West Prussia in large numbers and settled in the cities. Altogether the newcomers totaled about 11,000 persons.

With one stroke of his pen Frederick abolished the whole Polish constitutional system. The *starostwie*[3] became crown

---

[2] At that time the lowermost Vistula had two main branches which diverged from each other at a 90° angle. Each had but one exit to the Baltic. The eastern segment, the "mouth" mentioned in the text, led into the Frisches Haff, present-day Zalew Wiślany, a sweetwater lagoon that faces [former] East Prussia and opens to the sea only on its extreme, northeastern margin. The meandering, western branch, the so-called Dead Vistula, comprises the old harbor of Danzig-Gdańsk. For a long time it was connected to

saltwater only by means of a canal (Neufahrwasser = new channel). This passage lies to the left of the Dead Vistula's original mouth, long blocked by wind- and wave-driven sands. The western portion of the river has been linked to the Baltic by two vertical cuts. The lagoon remains unchanged. — Ed.

[3] These were fiefs belonging to the national domain. The kings granted them on life tenure to important nobles (*starost* = elder) in return for military services. — Ed.

lands and were leased to German officials. The properties of the clergy were placed under state administration. The government retained half of their yield in payment of the land tax. As in East Prussia the nobility had to surrender 25 percent of its net profits to the fisc; the peasantry, 33 percent. Administration and the courts were also shaped according to the pattern of the older provinces ... The Noteć [Netze] was regulated and the Bydgoszcz (Bromberg) Canal built. This waterway, which joined the Noteć and the Brda (Brahe) and thus indirectly the Oder and the Vistula, opened up a continuous, east-west passage between the Central and Eastern provinces. Bydgoszcz also became the temporary headquarters of the Royal Maritime Trade Society (founded in 1772), the main function of which was to supply the province with French salt produced from seawater. Later this body developed into a commerical organization which promoted other state economic enterprises.

There was practically no primary school instruction in the countryside prior to 1772. The Polish *szlachta* had no interest in educating the agrarian population. Now, however, rural schools were built in vast numbers ..., including some that used Polish. In general the King was glad to have officials in Polish parts of the province speak the local language ... West Prussia is the best example of Frederick's immediate concern for popular education.

GERHART RITTER (1886–1967) spent most of his brilliant academic life at Freiburg. A somewhat paradoxical figure, he was chiefly interested in political history but did work in many different areas. Among his many titles is a biography of his martyred friend, the Resistance leader Dr. Carl Goerdeler. Ritter himself belonged to a Freiburg circle of intellectual opposition to Hitler. Meinecke's potent influence, admiration for the best aspects of the Prussian heritage, and strong identification with his own nationality are apparent in the portion of Ritter's Friderican biography that treats the Polish question.*

Gerhart Ritter

Rational Power Politics

"Gloomy, cold and hard, like a sunless winter day," so Frederick's biographer Koser described his hero after his return from the Seven Years' War. And certainly, the serene light of self-confidence which had gilded the days of Frederick's youth, the classic days of Rheinsberg and Sans Souci, no longer brightened the second half of his reign. An infinite amount of resignation and bitterness was now interlaced in each day's work for the state. All the more remarkable is the greatness of Frederick's actual achievement.

More than anything else, the foreign relations of the monarchy after the Seven Years' War seemed to warrant pessimism. Prussia had maintained her position as a great power; but she had lost her former allies and gained an implacable foe. The feeling of constantly being threatened never left the king—in contrast to his successors. This was the reason for his unceasing effort to increase the state treasury, and above all to strengthen the army, which soon after the Seven Years' War was raised to a first-line force of 200,000 men. The main danger, in Frederick's view, continued to be the enmity of Austria, which pressed on Prussia's newly acquired position like a heavy, practically irremovable mortgage (to use a well-known Bismarckian phrase). It was no longer possible to ease this burden by allying oneself either with France or

*From Gerhart Ritter, *Frederick the Great* (Berkeley, Calif.: University of California Press, 1968), pp. 184–195, translated by Peter Paret with a useful introduction. Reprinted by permission of The Regents of the University of California and Eyre & Spottiswoode (Publishers) Ltd.

Britain. A resumption of the former friendship with France after all that had occurred during the great war was out of the question, even though the fundamental antagonism of British and French policy, on which Frederick had once based his calculations, was not terminated by the peace of 1763. Prussia and France faced each other with deep reserve.

Prussia's alliance with England, on the other hand, had ended in shrill discord. Frederick did not intend to keep on playing the part of the continental satellite, who "pulled the chestnuts out of the fire" for the British Empire. His unwillingness was underscored by the events of 1761 and 1762, after which—exactly like Bismarck a century later—he lost faith in the ability of Great Britain's parliamentary form of government to pursue an alliance policy that could survive a change of ministry. Only one way remained open to avoid the threatening diplomatic isolation: an approach to Russia. Russia's defection from the Grand Coalition had saved Prussia; the "Kaunitz Coalition" of 1756 must under no circumstances be allowed to recur. Russia and Austria must be kept apart permanently.[1] Frederick was prepared to make considerable sacrifices to attain this goal.

But here too memories of the war interfered. Empress Catherine had risen to power by opposing her husband's Prussian alliance; in the first manifesto after her accession she declared the King of Prussia to be the "mortal enemy" of Russia. Even more worrisome was the fact

that in her restless ambition she threatened Europe's peace both in Poland an at the Turkish border. Full of dreams fo expanding her empire, counseled b ambitious soldiers and politicians, sh pressed toward the west and the south a the same time. Could it ever be to Fred erick's advantage to support such ven tures? Would Prussia's situatio deteriorate even further if the empres succeeded in bringing Poland completel under Russian influence? And if her am bitions really could be diverted towar Turkey and she became entangled with Austria, should Frederick bind himsel to support her in the possible militar conflict that might result? What was th Near Eastern question to the King o Prussia? Was it worth risking the bones o a single Pomeranian musketeer? Th Prussian monarchy stood in dire need o peace, and a Russian alliance made sens only if it served to prevent war. To main tain peace on the basis of an alliance with the most belligerent of European ruler would certainly require diplomatic ability of an extraordinary kind.

However, Frederick succeeded! An not only did he preserve the peace, h was also able to gain a large, strategically important province without striking a blow—solely through peaceful negotia tion. This accomplishment constitutes the strongest evidence of Frederick's diplomatic mastery, which was now at its peak Cautiously and ingeniously he advanced by calculated moves toward his goal. None of his ministers and diplomats, only the old king in person directed the game.

The Polish question provided the point of departure for his approach to Russia. Formerly a great power, Poland had for over a century been in a process of dissolution, caused principally by the quarrels, selfishness, and political delusions of her nobility. The European powers for

---

[1] The reference is to Count, later Prince Wenzel Kaunitz-Rietberg (1711–1794), Maria Theresa's state chancellor and (in practice) foreign minister, and to the Diplomatic Revolution which he brought about by reconciling the traditionally hostile Habsburgs and Bourbons. — Ed.

heir part had become accustomed to taking advantage of this state of anarchy. They nurtured it by every means of corruption, by direct and indirect intervention, and managed to stifle every attempt at reform, whether originating with the kings or the diets. Each of the major power blocs maintained its own party of Polish nobles, which made its appearance chiefly at the elections of the king. During the era of Louis XIV, France had played the main role of ally and protector; later, Peter the Great had made himself the real ruler of Poland. He ruthlessly exploited the country's internal conflicts during the Northern War, shrinking neither from bribery nor brute force, and succeeded in turning the defenseless country into a satellite of Russia. Poland's former importance as the eastern ally of France practically disappeared. Louis XV's attempt to restore and revitalize the old connections by having his father-in-law Stanislaus Leszynski elected king, was defeated by an alliance of Russia and Austria in the War of the Polish Succession, in which Prussia participated as an auxiliary of the Habsburgs. Crown Prince Frederick himself had taken part in the campaign in Austrian headquarters as a pupil of Prince Eugene. When the death of August III, the Saxon Elector, shortly after the end of the Seven Years' War again raised the question of Polish succession, Prussia—now no longer a satellite of the eastern monarchies, but a neighbor of considerable power—advanced her own claims. Frederick, unlike his father, could not afford to leave the settlement of the Polish question chiefly to Russia and Austria.

He was aware of Catherine's ambitious plans to complete Poland's submission to Russia by elevating her former lover, the Polish noble Poniatowski, to the throne. What this might mean for Prussia had been demonstrated during the Seven Years' War, when the Russian armies had used Polish territory as a base for their operations. From the days of Peter the Great, Russian troops had occupied Polish soil as the guarantors of Poland's freedom, or of her "fortunate anarchy," as Catherine called it. If Russian domination became even more entrenched, her position on the lower course of the Vistula would at any time enable her to separate East Prussia from the main body of the monarchy. Frederick's sole alternative lay between joining Russia in her interference in Polish affairs, or of impotently observing the dangerous colossus advance to the Prussian border, and possibly even intrude itself between the Prussian provinces. The idea of supporting the shaky gentry republic with an anti-Russian alliance would have been downright utopian. There was nothing left to support in Poland: at least nothing that was truly viable; any such effort would only have led to a new war without prospect of victory. Moreover, in Prussia too it was a traditional axiom of statecraft that Polish impotence worked to the advantage of all her neighbors.

On the whole, a Russo-Prussian alliance was far more important to Frederick than to Catherine. Nevertheless, by an extremely subtle combination of level-headed reserve and personal flattery, and by cleverly utilizing the conflicting interests of the major powers in the Polish question, he was able to steer Russian policy in the desired direction. He was considerably helped by the diplomatic skill of his brother, Prince Henry. In the end Catherine, whose candidate for the Polish throne had been rejected in Vienna and Paris, unwillingly agreed to secure Prussia's support in return for a formal defensive alliance. By the terms of the treaty of April 1764 the two countries recognized each other's territorial integrity; if one party were attacked it would call on its ally for military or financial assistance. Both powers henceforth appeared jointly as "protectors of Polish electoral freedom" and as patrons of Poniatowski.

Prussia had been saved from the dangers of isolation. What is more, an association had been initiated which proved to be the most durable of all alliances of the Prussian monarchy, outlasting every change in the European power constellation and surviving even recurring estrangements between the two states. Later, after the French Revolution, when the conservative eastern powers combined against the dangers which threatened from the liberal west, friendship with Russia practically became the basis of Hohenzollern foreign policy. Its particular advantage to Prussia, the rising power, was the strong backing the alliance provided against the might of the Habsburg Empire—so long as the Near Eastern question sustained continuous tension between Russia and Austria. Russia's and Prussia's common interest in keeping Poland weak, which had originated with Frederick, remained one of the strongest ties between the partners, down to Bismarck's time. Both the Near Eastern and the Polish questions, however, carried great dangers with them—especially in Frederick's day, when Russia was not yet the champion of conservatism, but comported herself like a conquering, warlike power. The possibility of Prussia being involved in oriental adventures which did not concern her has already been mentioned. It was even more difficult to prevent Russia's claim to domination of the Polish state—which Prussia now supported—from working to Prussia's disadvantage. Spheres of influence had to

be agreed on that would be advantageous to Prussia. For good reason Frederick carefully avoided giving the empress the impression that he was the weaker partner, who stood in need of help. Very soon he encountered a tendency in his new ally to treat Prussia as a mere vassal—an experience which was to be repeated frequently during the next century, and which finally caused Bismarck to seek a counterbalance to Russia's far too demanding friendship by means of a dual alliance with Austria.

The brutality of Russia's action in Poland surpassed the worst expectations. The Russian ambassador, Prince Repnin, behaved like a dictator. Poniatowski, after being elected king, refused to act as a mere tool of the empress and even tried, by agreement with all parties, to eliminate the calamitous *Liberum Veto* of the deputies in the central diet. In return, the empress tossed the concept of "freedom of religion" for non-Catholic denominations as a bone of contention among the parties, and had Repnin instigate a virtual revolution of the nobility. Threats, bribes, and the arrest of political leaders added to the pressure, until the "silent parliament" of 1768 decided on the retention of the old anarchical constitution. It was highly inconvenient for the King of Prussia to be associated as an ally in these crude procedures, which were condemned by all of Europe: at the very least, he would have preferred different methods. The situation became completely bewildering to him when armed Catholic "confederates" rebelled against Russian domination. Catherine ordered the movement crushed by her troops and as further reprisal engineered an uprising of Ukrainian peasants and Cossacks against the Polish nobility. What were the ultimate aims of this policy? It was high time to consider a definitive solution to the Polish question.

Frederick never had any doubts about the region of Poland in which Prussia was mainly interested. As early as 1731, in the letter to Natzmer [his chamberlain], he had discussed the necessity of gaining a solid corridor to link Pomerania and East Prussia. His political testaments repeated this idea more than once and elaborated on it—but as late as 1768 without the hope of acquiring, in one stroke and with the consent of the empress, all of what later was to become known as "West Prussia." In fact, he encountered a cool refusal when in 1769 he cautiously suggested a plan to her ministers by which the three neighboring powers would agree on the acquisition of certain Polish border provinces, and thus eliminate their conflict of interests. Catherine was not yet ready to share with others the booty that seemed secure in her grasp.

The situation became even more dangerous when France, in connection with the Polish dispute, instigated a war between Turkey and Russia. A series of rapid victories led to Russian control of the so-called Danube Principalities; her ascendancy in the east threatened to grow intolerable, and Austria's warnings of armed counteraction became more menacing. With deep apprehension Frederick foresaw the danger of being involved as Russia's ally in a new war against Austria, which would finally overturn the balance of power in the east, and was thus diametrically opposed to the true interests of Prussia. But in order to avoid losing his newly won friend, he had no alternative for the time being but to live up to the terms of the treaty. For years he reluctantly paid subsidies to Russia; if absolutely necessary he would even have been prepared to go to war with Turkey. He hoped this policy would establish his claim to important compensations in the future. For the present, however, his position was so weak that he voluntarily renewed the Russian treaty without stipulating anything for himself beyond the formal recognition of his hereditary claims to Ansbach-Bayreuth!

That is not to say that he did not try to improve his standing within the alliance. As Catherine's actions increasingly disturbed Europe, Paris and Vienna began to show new interest in the King of Prussia. Kaunitz, always the clever calculator, would have liked to entice him to quit the Russian alliance by means of such artful combinations as offers of Polish territory in return for recognition of future Austrian hereditary claims to Silesia if the male line of the Hohenzollern should become extinct. Not for a moment would Frederick consider such proposals, but he welcomed Vienna's approaches. Somewhat as Bismarck did later, he used them to bring pressure on Russia. Two meetings with Emperor Joseph II, his youthful admirer, and with Kaunitz, which otherwise produced no results, served the purpose of a demonstration. At the first meeting Frederick even drafted a kind of "Reinsurance Treaty" designed to protect him against Austria without loosening his ties with Russia.[2] At least the negotiations served to strengthen the force of Austria's threats to the Russian Court, particularly after Austria occupied a strip of land in Polish Galicia as security for "claims of compensation."

---

[2] The reference is to Bismarck's bilateral treaty with Russia (1887) which succeeded the "Three Emperors'" agreements of the preceding period and which coexisted with the more fundamental Austro-German Alliance of 1879.—Ed.

Now even Catherine, in conversations with the Prussian mediator, Prince Henry, began to talk about dividing Polish territory among the neighboring powers. Frederick reacted to the first word of this suggestion with disbelief and suspicion, and even rejected the idea. It was characteristic of his pessimism that Prince Henry actually had to convince him that the hour to fulfill his long-cherished wishes was at hand. Protracted and fluctuating negotiations, in which Prussia took a very strong line, were still required before Frederick achieved his aim of being given the border area of the lower Vistula, with access to the Baltic. The treaties of 1772, known as the first partition of Poland, which the Polish parliament ratified under pressure of Russian arms, granted Frederick the territories of Ermland [Warmia] and West Prussia [Pomerelia], without Danzig [Gdańsk] or Thorn [Toruń]. In physical extent, this amounted only to one-third of Russia's gain and one-half of Austria's. But in political terms Frederick was the greatest winner.

To Prussia, her new territory brought the fulfillment of an undeniable and long-felt political need; the others simply enlarged their areas. Catherine was deeply disappointed: contrary to all her wishes, she had been forced to share the Polish booty after all, and, in particular, to cede the mouth of the Vistula. Moreover, the peace treaty with Turkey, forced upon her by Austria's threats, had snatched the fruits of the Turkish war, the Danube Principalities, from her grasp. Still, for the time being the appetite of the Russian giant was satisfied. At the expense of Poland the peace of Europe was secured.

The territories taken in 1772 made up about one-quarter of the area of the Polish Republic. That an act of brutal violence had been committed was acknowledged even by the chief participants. Austria gained the province of Galicia, a mere appendage on the far side of the Carpathians without natural connection to the Danube basin, and Maria Theresa at first vehemently opposed this acquisition. She was frankly indignant, indeed profoundly unhappy, that her son had joined in the partition, for which his occupation of the border zones had in fact provided the ostensible cause. In her eyes it was robbery, pure and simple. She felt that the partition destroyed the greatest source of pride in her life—the fact that Austria had always been on the side of justice. In the end, however, she consented, for the sake of the European "equilibrium"—prompting Frederick's malicious comment: "she cries, but she takes." He himself quite openly admitted in his *History of the Partition* that the manifestoes claiming putative "legal titles" to Polish territory were sheer deception on the part of the annexing powers. On the other hand, he had nothing but scorn for Poland's aristocratic anarchy. He considered it to be "the worst government in Europe with the exception of Turkey," and compared the country's level of civilization to that of the American Indians. In the task of introducing European culture to his new acquisition he saw the only moral justification for his claim. And it must be said that although formally the treaties of 1772 clearly constituted an open act of violence, their result—so far as Prussia was concerned—was not founded on force alone.

Today German historiography should be able to renounce its traditional retort to Polish accusations, namely, that it was the political ineptitude of Poland, or at least of her governing elite, that bore the blame for the downfall of the Polish state. No doubt this view was not inaccurate. Even without Frederick's intervention Poland could not possibly have withstood Russia's thirst for conquest. The Gentry Republic had proved itself incapable of protecting the states and culture of Europe against Russian encroachment. But we readily admit that the political downfall of this old and proud society was not solely a matter of "guilt," due entirely to the political and economic failings of a thoroughly corrupt aristocracy. As Stein shortly afterwards said with genuine sympathy, it was equally a matter of "misfortune," of extremely unfavorable geographic and political conditions. No one, however, can believe that the anarchic regime of the Polish nobility was able to contribute to the economic and intellectual life of the country even a fraction of what Frederick and his successors achieved in West Prussia. If a historical claim can be earned by constructive effort, the Prussian monarchy is surely entitled to it. Despite the harsh means employed, West Prussia's modernization—the replacement of primitive conditions by orderly government, a reliable legal system, and a sound economy—belongs among the brilliant achievements of Frederician administration.

[German historians] . . . have justly pointed out that the events of 1772 did not constitute a true "partition" of Poland. The three powers annexed border territories that the Polish state was unable to defend, a process recurring throughout history, which Germany in particular has frequently experienced without anyone calling it "partition." Poland's true partition, that is, her annihilation as a state, did not occur for another twenty years, in political conditions that had completely changed. National annihilation was never in Frederick's thoughts. For a time after the loss of its outlying areas, the Polish body politic even seemed to revive and regain its internal strength. Count Hertzberg, the Prussian minister of foreign affairs during Frederick's last years and under Frederick William II, strongly wanted to support these efforts at reform in order to avert a total breakup, which he felt would be a misfortune for Prussia as well as for Poland. We should be careful, therefore, not to evaluate the acquisition of West Prussia in the same light as the outcome of the so-called second and third partitions of 1793 and 1795, in which Prussia, frightened by the prospect of Russia's ascendancy, annexed much more territory than she could accommodate.

It is even less advisable to regard these events from the nineteenth-century point of view. The era before the French Revolution still knew nothing of the right of ethnic groups to self-determination. Even Napoleonic France was not noted for its hesitation in imposing the most arbitrary governmental boundaries on the peoples of Europe. Only in one sense, but that a highly significant one, were the three so-called partitions of Poland related. As Maria Theresa clearly perceived—and as Friedrich Gentz was later to argue in a famous pamphlet—this was the first time the monarchies of the *ancien régime* collaborated in a revolutionary act. We must repeat, it was an act in the ultimate consequences of which Frederick did not participate; but he did help pave the way for it. The degradation, and finally the annihilation by brute force, of a realm which, though it was extremely weak, nevertheless was ancient and venerable in history, the ruthless destruction of historical rights for the sake of sheer political convenience, the overthrow of the traditional European balance of power by the forcible elimination of one of its members—all this is touched by the breath of a new revolutionary age, an age in which political authority is no longer based on historic tradition and divine right, but on concepts of political expediency and on cool, irreverent rationality.

HERBERT H. KAPLAN (b. 1932), a recipient of numerous academic honors, teaches at the University of Indiana, a major center of Eastern European studies. His continued interest in eighteenth-century Russia's international role is reflected in *The First Partition of Poland* (1962), from which the following selection is taken, and in a second work, *Russia and the Outbreak of the Seven Years' War* (1968). As a specialist in diplomatic affairs, Kaplan is deeply involved with foreign ministry records and other primary sources that provide good evidence for advocates of the power-equilibrium theory of history.*

Herbert H. Kaplan

Prince Henry and the Balance of Power

"The King of Prussia has given his consent and I hear that Prince Henry will accordingly set out some time this [September] from the Court of Sweden for Petersburg. There are people who pretend that Prince Henry has no real business either in Sweden or Russia, but that it is a journey of mere ostentation and meant to give occupation to the speculative politicians."

But Henry had "real" business at both courts, and it was somewhat Machiavellian in character. Henry saw the confusion in Europe as a chance for Prussia to profit —perhaps even to divide up the Germanies between Austria and Prussia. He hoped at least that Prussia might gain some territory out of Europe's difficulties.

Frederick did not agree with his brother. He believed himself too old for another military adventure, and he did not think Austria financially sound enough to do anything to help. Nevertheless, the first opportunity for bringing about Henry's wishes came when he was invited to St. Petersburg.

It would be more truthful to say that Henry invited himself there—Catherine merely fulfilled his wish. He believed that by going to St. Petersburg he could further his plans for aggrandizement and that Catherine would help him. Most assuredly, this was for Henry the "boldest stroke" of his life. "Unable to induce the King to take even the first steps toward the seizure of West Prussia, he had de-

*From Herbert H. Kaplan, *The First Partition of Poland* (New York: Columbia University Press, 1962), pp. 131–146. Extensive citations of documentary sources omitted.

cided to take them himself and virtually to make Prussia a present of the provinces." Immediately after Henry learned of his mission to Sweden he arranged to have Golitsyn [an influential Russian nobleman] inform the Russian court that Prince Henry of Prussia would be very grateful for an invitation to visit St. Petersburg. Frederick had no knowledge of Henry's negotiations for getting himself invited to the Russian court.

On July 30 Catherine wrote to Frederick that she would be greatly pleased if Henry, after his sojourn in Sweden, could spend some time with her in Russia. She suggested several means of travel by which Henry could make the trip to St. Petersburg and offered everything at her disposal to make his trip and stay in Russia enjoyable.

From the standpoint of Russia, a visit from Henry would be desirable for several reasons. First, Frederick had already had one meeting with Joseph and a second was forthcoming (September 3–7) [1770]; these would serve to bring the two German courts closer together. Russia could not afford to have her alliance with Frederick weakened or possibly replaced by an Austrian one. A meeting with Henry would in a sense replace a meeting with Frederick, since it was believed at the Russian court that Henry had considerable influence with his brother. Furthermore, Catherine was anxious to learn what had happened in Sweden.

Frederick informed Henry that Catherine "requests you with so much eagerness" that he could not refuse. To Catherine he poetically wrote: "Neither the sea, nor the heights, nor the precipice will stop [Henry], and he will overcome all the obstacles . . . to present homage to You, Madam." He went on to applaud Catherine's greatness and to express his thankfulness at being her ally. He pictured "Constantinople trembling at the sight of the Russian fleet and the Sultan forced to sign the peace which Your moderation will dictate to him."

Nearly three weeks later, after he had had time to send Henry a special cipher that would be used only by him, Frederick was able to speak his mind more clearly on the subjects most important to him. Sweden, of course, held a claim on Frederick's attention; he wanted to reestablish the best relations between Catherine and his sister, the Queen. But of more immediacy, he desired to bring about the end of the Russo-Turkish War and the pacification of Poland. Henry was informed of the Neustadt discussions[1] and the Turkish request for mediation. Henry was told to influence Catherine toward a moderate policy with the Turks and the Poles. If Catherine were to show clemency after so many victories, this not only would assure a good and solid peace but would add to Catherine's fame. The Russian court must accept the mediation of Austria and Prussia and not make "untenable conditions" to the Poles. Catherine had to reduce the demands which she had made at the last Diet, otherwise the troubles would never end in Poland. If she would do this, Austria and Prussia would help in bringing the Confederates to "reason, and then the peace would be stable."

Henry arrived in St. Petersburg on October 12. Several days later he wrote Frederick that every day he had been having "familiar conversations with the Empress, and, as M. [Gregory] Orlov has a higher position here than one can imagine, I am confident that . . . I shall be able to use him."[2] He talked to Panin [Russia's foreign minister] who told him

---

[1] The reference is to the talks of September 3–7. The town was in the Principality of Jägerndorf.—Ed.

[2] Orlov was a Guards officer and one of Catherine's favorite lovers, possibly also the murderer of her husband, the childish Tsar Peter III.—Ed.

that Catherine desired the pacification of Poland, that Volkonskii [Russian ambassador to Poland] had already been advised to negotiate with the nobles of the Commonwealth, that the Dissidents would yield in their demands, and that an accommodation would be reached with the Confederates. Panin explained that "his sovereign desired the peace, that she hoped to have it, and that she worked for it."

When Frederick received Catherine's letter of October 9, which, according to him, neither refused nor accepted the mediation, he wrote Henry: "I am resolved not to meddle either in the peace or in the affairs of Poland and to be only a simple spectator of events; while those people there are able to accept or refuse us as mediators, it is not necessary that they openly mock us."

As the days passed Frederick became more irritable and more pronounced in his views.

The whole Kingdom [of Poland] is alienated from the Russians. If the Empress of Russia believes she has partisans, she deceives herself very much. The question is to pacify these troubles. If the peace imposes laws that the Poles believe they are not obliged to observe, [the troubles] will begin again in three months. I ought to add another consideration. The court of Vienna regards the affairs of Poland with the greatest discontent; and, although I hesitate to say it, if the Russians, after the peace is made, do not recall their troops from this kingdom, then the Austrians, in the end, will become impatient.

. . . Russia should make a tolerable pacification plan for Poland and communicate it to me and to the court of Vienna. If this plan is found reasonable—that is to say, in maintaining the King on the throne and compromising a little on the other [formerly announced demands]—I should be able to convince the court of Vienna to reprimand, jointly with me, the Confederates and force them to submit. That would provide a stable peace and a

new reign. But the Empress does not wish to follow my advice. I fear that sooner or later the smoldering fire will ignite a blaze which will devour all Europe.

Besides, I renounce the title of mediator.

Henry, as yet unaware of Frederick's change of mind, urged the pacification of Poland before peace was made with the Porte. He suggested a general confederation which would command the obedience of the malcontents and further suggested that the Austrians would assist in this venture. He was informed by the Russian court that, although Russia would welcome the idea of Frederick's encouraging the Austrians to engage themselves in this action, she did not want that power "meddling directly in the affairs of Poland."

Henry's idea was not new. Russia had for some time been trying to effect such a policy. Whether her new attempt was influenced by Henry's suggestion is not known, but she tried again. Russia as before, was not successful. Nevertheless, this new failure revealed the lack of trust the Poles had for the promises of the Russians.

Wroughton [British resident in Poland] reported that Volkonskii "received a refusal from every quarter he has applied to." The Potockis [a great Polish noble family] told Volkonskii:

Their family had been notoriously deceived at Radom, where with bayonets at their throats, they had been obliged to sign the General Confederation [1767], on conditions quite contrary to those, on which they had undertaken it, on the most solemn engagements with Russia; that having been thus forced to acts, which had driven the Nation to their present state of despair, and failed in their engagements to their friends, and society, they now saw the difficulty, if not the impossibility, of the Nation's trusting again the promises of Russia; that as to their promising in order to ruin the Czartoryskis, it was true their family were long rivals, and even enemies, but, if Russia was capable of acting thus violently with people, whose greatest crime with the Nation was for forty years past having been connected with the Court, what hopes could new friends have, of being treated better, whenever their conscience should put them under the necessity of refusing to comply with every demand of that power; that likewise it would be deceiving Russia to make her believe that the affairs of the Dissidents could possibly be maintained.

During the remaining weeks of November nothing significant took place in the negotiation between the two northern courts. At the same time that Frederick announced that if the war continued between Russia and the Porte he would not continue the subsidies, Panin informed Henry that very soon the Russian court would present a definite program concerning the war and the pacification of Poland.

Early in December the Vienna court formally proclaimed the reincorporation of Spisz [Spiš] into the Crown of Hungary. It was the beginning of the dismemberment of Poland. Whatever plans Russia and Prussia might have had for Poland would have to be adjusted to this fact.

Within the next two weeks, reports came from Vienna and Warsaw describing the advance of the cordon of Imperial Eagles and other acts of incorporation into the Crown of Hungary of the territory already occupied by Austrian troops. The Austrian court claimed more territory extending to Austrian Silesia and including no less than nine towns and ninety-seven villages. The inhabitants of this area would be treated as subjects of the Empress-Queen, and they would not pay more taxes now than they had before.

The Prussian court did not at first show any concern: "I do not regard of great consequence," Frederick wrote to Rohd

[Prussian ambassador to Austria], "the seizure on the frontiers of that republic by the court where you are. . . . I am persuaded rather that once the peace is made, she will not delay in abandoning this possession and confine herself to her boundaries *ante bellum*."

Golitsyn, however, told Rohd that his court would not view the Austrian seizure with indifference. During the first week of 1771 one discussion followed the other at Petersburg concerning the Austrian court's seizure. Solms [Prussian ambassador to Russia] wrote to Frederick on January 8 that the Russian court believed that "if Austria gave the example for the dismemberment of Poland, Your Majesty and the Empress of Russia would not be wrong in doing the same; that in the archives in Berlin and Petersburg could easily be found the right to lay claim to the Bishopric of Warmia [Ermland] for Your Majesty and to Polish Livonia [northern Latvia] for Russia." Russia would then extend her boundaries along the Dwina (Dvina) as far as Polock; and if a line were to be drawn as far as the Dnieper, the incorporation of the territory lying on the eastern side of those two rivers would give Russia her "natural" boundaries. This would be considered a just compensation for the six years of war in Poland and with the Turks. Prussia would receive by her acquisition an adequate recompense for the expenses she had suffered during this time in fulfilling the alliance with Russia. "The removal of these provinces from Poland," Solms continued, would not, according to the Russian court, "render her king less able or less recognized than he had been." From the Russian side, this proposition was, in general, the substance of the secret project which General Chernyshev had submitted in 1763.

On the evening of January 8, Henry was

approached directly by those at the Russian court who favored this revolutionary change in Russian policy toward Poland.

This evening I have been with the Empress, who told me in fun that the Austrians were seizing two starostas [administrative units] in Poland and that they have placed Imperial troops on the frontiers of those starostas. She added: "But why does not everyone take such action?" I replied that although You, my very dear brother, have a cordon drawn in Poland, You have not occupied the starostas. "But," the Empress said smiling, "why not occupy them?" A moment later, Count Chernyshev approached me and spoke to me on the same subject, adding: "But why not occupy the Bishopric of Warmia? It is necessary, after all, that everyone have something."

Although this was only a discourse of pleasantries, it is certain that it had a purpose, and I have no doubt that it will be possible for You to profit from this occasion. Tomorrow Count Panin comes to my house. I shall tell him what You have written me on the subject of the Austrians.

It is perhaps significant that not only Chernyshev (who had long been an advocate of extending the frontier of Russia into Poland) but now also Catherine favored the idea of dismemberment. It meant that Panin's influence over Catherine in foreign affairs was waning again, as it had after the outbreak of the Russo-Turkish War and with Volkonskii's succession at Warsaw. It meant, moreover, that the "Northern System" was being discarded.

But Panin opposed any idea of partition and made this clear to Solms and Henry. "He is very much against the imitation of [the Austrian seizure]," Solms wrote to Frederick on January 11. If anything were to be done, Panin told Solms, it should be made known that the King of Prussia and the Empress of Russia oppose such ideas. Panin would "never give his

sovereign counsel to seize for herself that which did not belong to her."

There was an apparent division in the Russian advisory council. "All those who are supporting aggrandizement wish that everyone would take something in order that Russia might profit at the same time, whereas Count Panin is for tranquillity and peace." Henry, of course, wanted Frederick to involve himself in the partition. "I believe You risk nothing in seizing something for Yourself," he urged his brother; a "plausible pretext" could be found to seize the Bishopric of Warmia.

The influence of the "partition" party at the Russian court was soon felt in other quarters. Volkonskii told Benoit [Prussian resident in Poland] that he desired very much that Vienna persist in occupying Polish territory, and that Frederick and Catherine both agree to dismembering Poland. But Frederick was still not convinced that the seizure by the Vienna court would be permanent. "I believe," he wrote to Benoit on January 23, "that [Maria Theresa] only did it in order to keep the states of Hungary safe against the plague and that the intention of the Imperial Court is not to try to appropriate the starostas." But there was a change in Frederick's tone when he wrote to Solms the same day: "If they pretend to keep them, they surely authorize the other neighbors of Poland to think about declaring their rights to do the same." But he believed there was sufficient time to think about such things.

On the following day he wrote to his brother, saying that he would not give "six sous in order to acquire" the Bishopric of Warmia. Besides, it was an "unpardonable mistake in politics ... to contribute to the aggrandizement of [Russia], who will be able to become a dreadful and appalling neighbor for all

Europe." Frederick considered the conclusion of the Russo-Turkish War the most important work that had to be done, and the affairs of Poland nothing more than "trifles."

However, on January 31, after having received a report that the Vienna court was massing 30,000 troops along the Hungarian frontier, Frederick seemed interested in the idea of obtaining Polish land, but he was convinced that Panin's view would stand the test of all criticism. He wrote Henry: "Concerning the matter of the seizure of the Duchy of Warmia, I am abstaining because the game is not worth much. This piece is [cut] so thin that it would not compensate for the clamors that it would excite; but Polish Prussia, even excluding Gdańsk [Danzig], would be worth the trouble, for we will have the Vistula and free communication with the kingdom [of Prussia]."

The reports about Austrian troop movements continued. Calls were sent out by the Austrian court to Italy and the Low Countries. Rohd rightly interpreted this move as having a double intention—to frighten Russia into not extending her conquests and to add force to the extension of the Austrian cordon in Poland.

Frederick was still not overly disconcerted by Austria's activities; he believed that they would "accelerate rather the reestablishment of peace between Russia and the Porte." He did not believe that the "small parcels" of territory that the Vienna court had taken possession of in Poland were of "much consequence." However, he felt that if Austria formally incorporated these territories [the incorporating had already taken place], the neighboring powers would be able to follow her example and similarly renew some old claims on Polish territory.

Everything changed when Henry re-

turned home. He left St. Petersburg at the end of January and arrived in Berlin on February 17. The following day he went to Potsdam, where he stayed the week—persuading Frederick of the necessity for partitioning Poland. In the words of Chester Easum, who has written an excellent biography of Henry: "No other of his servants was ever able to persuade Frederick to reverse himself so completely or so suddenly on a matter of such major importance; and none was ever permitted, even temporarily, so to take play out of the King's hands."[3]

Frederick's change of policy is significantly noted in his letter to Solms on February 20.

The seizure which the Austrians have made along the frontiers of Hungary ... appears sufficiently interesting to merit the attention of neighboring powers.... The court of Vienna has already exercised several acts of sovereignty. Prince Kaunitz has answered the complaints of the republic of Poland in a vague manner, and he clearly indicates the intention of [the Vienna court] to assert its ancient rights....

To several persons at the court of Russia, the news of this seizure gave birth to the idea that all of Poland's neighbors could make similar seizures....

The real issue is to preserve Poland in its entirety, but since the Austrians wish to dismember one part, [it is necessary] to prevent this dismemberment from upsetting the balance of power between Austria and Prussia. ... I see no other means ... than to imitate the example that the court of Vienna has given me; to assert my ancient rights, which my archives will furnish me; and to take some small province of Poland. This will make the Austrians desist in their enterprise, or, if they wish to assert their pretentious claims, it will restore [the balance of power]. ... An acquisition of this nature would not give umbrage to

---

[3] For Easum, see Suggestions for Further Reading (under "General").

anyone; only the Poles have the right to cry, but their behavior does not merit either Russia's or my sympathy. Once the Great Powers are in accord and work for pacification, they will not be checked. . . .

Above all, I would wish to know the true sentiment of the court of Russia on this affair. . . . If you succeed in making the Empress and her ministers see my point of view, you will render me a service. [It is] the only way to maintain equality between my [court] and the court of Vienna.

A week later Frederick wrote Solms that he was convinced that only force would make Austria desist from occupying Polish territory. But Frederick did not want war. At the same time, Finckenstein and Hertzberg, Frederick's two trusted and reliable ministers of state, were requested to investigate the claims the Prussian court could make on Poland with regard to pretensions in general, districts that would be convenient for the King of Prussia to annex, and the necessary means for bringing this affair to a happy ending.

The ministerial reply was disheartening. It presented Frederick with an uncertain legal pretension. "Your Majesty will see by this memoir that the pretensions of the house of Brandenburg on Poland are neither important nor strong." But Frederick would not let that bother him. He agreed with his ministers that the most advantageous acquisition would be Pomorze (Pomerania) and the land extending along the River Noteć [Netze] as far as the Vistula. But if this should fail, equal compensations should be found on the other side of the Vistula, for example, Malbork (Marienburg),[4] Chelmno (Kulm), and the Bishopric of Warmia [Ermland]. The example of the court of

Vienna's seizure would be followed. A cordon would first be drawn as a means for taking into possession the desired territory, and then a vague explanation of the pretensions would be made to support the occupation. "If the Russians and the Austrians take their part, [the Poles] will not be able to cry more against one than the other, and besides their clamors are powerless." Frederick instructed his ministers to draw up a statement of these pretensions and have it sent to the court of Russia.

The detailed statement, drawn up and presented on March 5, drew from Frederick the simple but precise comment: "This piece is good." Finckenstein and Hertzberg had worked hard; they found that Frederick could also claim territories in Posnań [Posen], Oświęcim [Auschwitz], Zator, and Siewierz. They gave Frederick a brief that explained the strategy and tactics, the objections which should be anticipated, and the necessity for a flexible policy.

The ambitious and hard-working ministers at Berlin found their counterpart in Solms, who displayed a never-ending determination to win Panin over to the idea of partitioning Poland. Panin was the only minister at St. Petersburg who still opposed the idea, but he was also the most influential. Solms discerned, however, that Panin was weakening under the pressure of those who desired the partition, especially Chernyshev and Orlov. "There are persons who have stated in the Council that Russia ought to imitate these examples [of Austria] and who are only leading Count Panin step by step to convincing himself that he should no longer oppose the dismemberment of Poland." Panin, according to Solms, did not deny the rights of the Prussian court to certain territories in Poland, but only raised doubts and objections to the man-

---

[4] Formerly the fortified seat of the Grand Masters of the Teutonic Order.—Ed.

ner of executing them. Panin hoped that Frederick would defer for some time the execution of the partition. The principal reason for such a request was that Russia would be totally embarrassed if she were to agree upon a scheme of partition that would violate every promise and treaty that she had made with the Commonwealth.

But once Frederick had committed himself to the idea of partition, he was unwavering. He challenged every argument Panin offered. He wrote to Solms on March 24, "I know very well that [Russia] has given her assurance that she will help preserve in entirety the provinces of that kingdom. But after the Confederates have openly taken arms against her, it seems to me that Poland would not deserve this kind of guarantee." It would not be difficult to justify a change in Russia's policy toward Poland if Russia was reminded that the Russo-Turkish War arose from the anarchy which persisted in Poland. Since the Austrian court had seized Polish territory and was not likely to relinquish it, were not Russia and Prussia obliged to restore the balance of power? Moreover, if the Prussian alliance was worth having, should not Russia do everything to keep it?

Panin did not change his mind, but it became increasingly difficult for him to repeat his former statements and yet remain on a good footing with Frederick. He needed time, and he requested that Frederick find out the intentions of the Austrian court regarding the occupation of Polish territory. The urgency of the situation increased when reports circulated that Austria had continued her policy of entrenchment in Poland and her massing of troops along the Hungarian frontier.

The visit of Prince Henry to Russia and the subsequent negotiations between the Prussian and Russian courts added to the rumors at Vienna that a partition of Poland was afoot. These rumors alarmed Kaunitz. "What causes us most worry is the very suspicious Russian and Prussian aggrandizement schemes in Poland," Kaunitz informed Lobkowitz, the Austrian ambassador to Russia. Austria, therefore, must thwart "such extremely dangerous plans," and "let the King of Prussia know, politely but firmly, that we will not be indifferent to his designs of aggrandizement." Kaunitz was fearful that "an open rupture" might result between the three powers.

This was sheer hypocrisy. Austria had been the first to incorporate Polish land and by moving troops into Hungary had not diminished but increased the possibility of "an open rupture" between the three powers. Notwithstanding the fact that Kaunitz was speaking for the Vienna court, and there was never a question of his loyalty, he did not favor his court's embarking on this policy. Even after Austria had launched the policy, Kaunitz attempted to dissuade his court from executing it. Because of this attitude, it is sometimes difficult to distinguish between his personal feelings and court policy. A good example is his letter of April 10 to Swieten, the new Austrian envoy to the Prussian court: "As soon as peace between Russia and the Porte is established; Poland pacified and her future peace guaranteed by the Empress of Russia, the King of Prussia, and our court; and when the King of Prussia and Russia have withdrawn their troops from that kingdom, then will also their Imperial and Royal Majesties withdraw their army to restore the occupied territory."

On the other hand, it may be argued that Kaunitz only said this to impress the Prussian court (and therefore also the Russian court) that Austrian acquisitions in Poland were merely temporary and that no corresponding action should be taken from their side. It is also not unknown that an envoy has been kept in the dark about the exact nature of his court's policy in order to deceive the court where he was. However, Kaunitz' brief to Maria Theresa on April 18 seems to support his opposition to Austria's Polish policy. He stated his opposition to the Austrian incorporation of the Polish districts because the Austrian claim was not proved valid. The only reason that Austria occupied these districts was to safeguard her own frontiers, and until the claims for incorporation could be proved beyond a doubt nothing should have been done. He insisted, but was unsuccessful in convincing his mistress, that the governor of the districts be called *Administrator Districtuum Territorii*, rather than *Administrator Provinciae Reincorporatae*. Furthermore, in order not to whet Frederick's appetite, Kaunitz also suggested that the income derived from these districts during the occupation be turned over to Andrzej Poniatowski, a General in the Austrian army, but also the brother of the King of Poland.

In any event, Kaunitz was fighting a losing battle not only with his court but with Prussia, and at the Russian court Panin was the only important minister who wanted to preserve Polish territorial integrity.

But, for the moment, there was nothing to fear from Frederick, because as usual he would not make a move without the consent and advice of Russia. On April 24 he wrote to Solms: "But as to my taking possession [of Polish land] Count Panin can be certain that I shall undertake this only after there is perfect accord with his court." However, if Austria increased her holdings in Poland, this might be just enough to persuade Panin that it was necessary that his court join in the spoils. "Search in your archives and see if you will not find titles to something more than that which you have already occupied," Frederick told Swieten on April 27, "to some palatinate that should be pleasing to you; believe me, it is necessary to profit from this occasion; I also shall take my part and Russia hers."

The first major change came in May. Solms wrote to Frederick on the seventeenth: "I regard the matter of an acquisition by Your Majesty in Poland as something that will encounter no more obstacles here." On May 27 Panin for the first time reported to the Council the suggestions and requests of Frederick for the acquisition of Polish land. Panin stated that "in consequence of the news of the seizure by the Vienna court of Polish starostas on the Hungarian frontier, the King of Prussia told this court that he does not intend to be a peaceful spectator of such an act." Frederick, Panin continued, "also has the right to adjacent possessions of Polish land and intends to take them; if Russia also has such demands and wants to profit from the opportunity, she could act in common cause with him." Here was the opportunity for the "fulfillment of all the desires" of Russia. In a general way Panin outlined the provinces that would devolve upon the two courts. Prussia would get what she wished (except Gdańsk [Danzig]), and Russia would extend her frontiers westward to include Polish Livonia. The Council agreed.

LUDWIG DEHIO (1888–1963), a native East Prussian, spent the greater portion of his career as an archivist in Berlin. In 1946 he became director of the Marburg State Archives and professor of modern history at the local university. From 1949 on he was also editor of *Historische Zeitschrift*. His two major works, *The Precarious Balance: Four Centuries of the European Power Struggle* and *Germany and World Politics in the Twentieth Century* appeared in 1948 and 1955, respectively. Dehio emphatically rejects what he considers Prussia's militaristic heritage, but he is at one with Ritter, the object of his critique, in accepting *raison d'état* as a key factor in the operation of history.*

Ludwig Dehio

Militaristic Raison d'État

Is it wrong to render the verdict "guilty of militarism" in the case of Frederick the Great who so openly confessed his motives for attacking Silesia and who waged war on its account for more than a decade? Ritter himself occasionally notes that militarism is especially characteristic of powers that are trying to break out of narrow confines, and eighteenth-century Prussia definitely falls into this category.

Let us summarize Ritter's interpretation at the outset: Frederick was no militarist. As the author of *Historical Profile* marshals his evidence, proceeding from one argument to another, he manages to create mounting tension in the reader's mind. We must be satisfied, however, with emphasizing his main ideas. When all is said and done, they amount to an examination of the relationship, if any, between the two concepts of *raison d'état* and militarism. Ritter is concerned with proving that the King, despite his Silesian adventure, never broke the rules of genuine *raison d'état*. But, since . . . this phenomenon is associated with a lasting state of peace, Ritter must lump together such features of Frederick's reign as will enable us to ascertain the existence of pacific aims in his dealings both with his own subjects and with foreign powers.

Naturally it is easier to find positive evidence in the domestic arena. For surely the monarch's humane, Enlightened ideals are quite apparent when we

*From Ludwig Dehio, "Um den deutschen Militarismus," *Historische Zeitschrift,* CLXXX (1955), 52–57. Translated by Thomas M. Barker.

consider the attention he paid to legal affairs, the economy, and population growth and when we recall his efforts to protect the citizenry as much as possible from military burdens in both peace and war and to spare his people the expenses of maintaining the Court. Ritter believes that reason of state has an obviously peaceful and ethical character with respect to all these realms of activity, and he blames Borussian historiography[1] for having glorified his hero's military deeds and for having caused his civilian accomplishments to fade somewhat into the background.

Ritter encounters greater difficulty in seeking to show that in the last analysis foreign policy also served to guarantee a lasting state of peace within his particular meaning of *raison d'état*. The reign encompassed four wars even though, as the writer remarks, they claimed hardly more than ten of its forty-six years. Of course, if one is willing to concede this point, the reproach of militarism—as Ritter understands the word—is groundless. The greatest hurdle that has to be overcome in this context is the invasion of Silesia in 1740. To be sure, the fact is stressed that Frederick made careful, rational calculations beforehand. Yet is all of this proof *per se* of ethically motivated attempts to achieve a lasting state of peace? On occasion Ritter even calls the war a brilliant improvisation, a bold policy of conquest, and an adventure. There can be no quarrel at all about royal motives, for he does not bother to dispute the view that Frederick's aggression evoked a chain reaction, namely, the later, seven-year struggle for bare existence in which the persistence of the hero approached "the limits of what was still

politically sensible." But! "As the ultimate success demonstrated," so we are informed in one of the most revealing paragraphs of the book, "the firm belief of the King that his opponents would finally wear out proved to be genuine reason of state" (that is, after the unexpected death of the Tsarina had weakened the coalition). Genuine *raison d'état* as evinced by ultimate success, in short. Frederick's acquittal from the charge of militarism! Ritter goes on to explain that there can be no question of blind recklessness since the monarch longed to be in Sans Souci cultivating the muses while he was conducting his campaigns. Frederick was not aiming at the annihilation of his opponents and did not pervert the defensive character of the Seven Years' War by indulging in fantasies of conquest. Moreover, he acquired Polish territory by diplomatic methods, shied away from new wars, and devoted himself to strengthening the internal resources of the realm. A lasting state of peace here too and Prussia a country that "guaranteed peace"! Such is the net result of the passages under review.

Who will not hear the arguments—sketched but roughly here—in defense of Ritter's hero without experiencing a feeling of respect for their passionately patriotic proponent? But will there not also be many who will wish to question their validity? Let us allude to at least some doubts. First, pacific objectives: even though one can scarcely deny the idealistic mentality of the protagonist (a secondary motive), his efforts hardly ever went further than what was immediately useful. As far as military deeds are concerned, the refusal to press for destruction of Prussia's main enemies was dictated by restrictions upon the state's resources. On the other hand, there *was* an attempt to eliminate a lesser foe,

---

[1] The reference is to the pre-1914 school of nationalist historians.—Ed.

Saxony. Yet all this is merely a side issue when compared with the question of whether the assault upon Silesia was really part and parcel of ethical *raison d'état,* despite Frederick's own very trenchant revelations, or whether this act was not an instance of an irrational, predatory leap beyond the bounds of any *raison d'état* at all, not merely the kind operative in Prussia at that time but the type that Ritter postulates? Not everyone will be satisfied with the final success of 1763 as an answer. The fatal thought occurs: what if Elizabeth had not died at the right moment, and what if ruin—the destiny of Charles XII of Sweden—had been the result of persisting "to the very margins of what still made sense." Ritter admits that the Northern ruler was a "militarist." While Frederick's intellectualism would prevent historians from dismissing him as a militarist of the same ilk as his Swedish counterpart, would the Prussian monarch not be considered to have finally fallen victim to a military mistake made at the beginning of his reign? It is difficult to see how he could have escaped such judgment by posterity. Thus success is shown to be the dividing line between ethical reason of state and blind militarism. Again and again one is reminded of Hegel, who regarded a favorable outcome as the sole justification of an action. Apparently the vanquished do not find it quite as easy to invoke ethical reason of state as do conquerors. Let us note parenthetically that the great militarists most often cited by Ritter are always simultaneously the losers, that is, those who have been politically outmaneuvered, men such as Louis XIV, Charles XII, Napoleon, and, later on, Ludendorff and Hitler.

It is well known that Frederick himself spoke in authoritative fashion about his understanding of *raison d'état.* Is Ritter's idea of ethical reason of state really based upon royal pronouncements? In my opinion the unprejudiced reader of the political testaments of Frederick the Great cannot help but see how the bright glow of morality becomes ever dimmer, although Ritter believes that he can discern such luminosity both with regard to *raison d'état* in general and its Friderican manifestation in particular. For, after all, in these documents peace is made subject to the merciless laws of preparing for battle. The use of military means is viewed not only defensively but also offensively—for example, the Saxon plan—in the event of a "just" war, that is, whenever one fights to exalt and aggrandize the state and not simply because of the personal caprices of the ruler. And this is what we are supposed to regard as ethical? To speak of "rounding-off" territory—one may ask whether the acquisition of Silesia actually made the state rounder—is to employ a rather delicate expression for the House of Brandenburg's ambition to become one of the premier powers of Europe. To be sure, if expansion could have been achieved without the actual use of weapons, that is, merely by saber rattling as in the instance of the Polish tidbit, then the maintenance of peace would have been agreeable to Frederick too. But only in such a case! In any event, it would be a Sisyphean labor of artificial interpretation if one were to prove that the compass needle of Prussian reason of state pointed directly to a lasting state of peace rather than simply to the "interest" of the state in its own growth by means of a super-dimensional emphasis upon armaments. Even a moral justification of Prussian expansionism from the standpoint of reshaping obsolete legal conditions within the conquered areas meets with difficulty.

Although one may think today that Frederick's victories did away with anachronisms, he did not see fit to utilize such argumentation in defense of his actions. He was not at all certain about the beneficial effects of his conquests for the Prussian people. Not for one moment did he gloss over the fact that the whole area of foreign policy has nothing to do with private morality—something which he considered unfortunate, at least in theory. In any case, his personal rationalist ethics and the everyday traffic rules of relations among states, not to mention the interests of his own country, simply diverged, at least "until a less benighted age will accord honorable behavior the place it deserves." How could reason of state, in Ritter's words "the radiant beam of the victorious power of human enlightenment," brighten this dark dissonance? After all, Frederick believed quite soberly that *raison d'état* was simply not ennobled by that ethical majesty which Ritter ascribes to it, least of all in foreign policy, the sphere of action most important to the King.

Admittedly, the polarity of Frederick's thought makes one hesitate before risking a final judgment of the problem in so few words. Meinecke's sensitive reading of all the evidence demonstrates this most clearly. Yet it is this scholar's work that leaves us in no doubt concerning the pole toward which Frederick's reason of state decidedly leaned. I find that Ritter is hardly able to shake these conclusions. Indeed, his morally elevated reason of state cannot be equated at all with Frederick's variety unless one resorts to sheer Procrustean methods. The pungent odor of a predatory animal again and again permeates the breezes of this lasting state of peace. More realistic, it seems, is the praise which Ritter's earlier biography accords the "prudent insight" of its hero,

"in particular the recognition that power is a natural phenomenon which resists pure intellectualization."

Ritter provides a unique kind of apologetic argumentation by comparing Frederick's wars with Europe's struggles for hegemony, especially the last one [World War II]. It is a comparison with Hitler, in fact, which brings to mind the temporal genesis of Ritter's ideas. What courage was necessary during the Third Reich to allow anything of this nature to echo, even remotely, in front of an audience! How disturbing an effect such reflections must have had at that time! But today the situation is quite different. We advise critically inclined foreigners not to judge our great statesmen with the yardstick of the present but by the standards of whatever period in the past one may be examining. Let us also keep the same advice in mind when defending these statesmen. It is not as if just any comparison were valid. Such an approach is admissible only as long as one carefully peels off the *tertium comparationis,* that is, after one has accounted for differences dictated by the passage of time. For example, the fact that Frederick, unlike Hitler, never engaged in total war becomes less significant when one considers how many reasons there were to keep him from doing so. No less indicative is the fact that after ten years of waging war over Silesia his main achievement was to preserve the original conditions of peace, in short, that he knew when to stop. In contrast to Hitler and his predecessors, the Prussian monarch was not involved in a war for hegemony with all its initial temptations and ultimate inevitabilities. Comparisons of simultaneous phenomena are far less susceptible to error. Of course one must not let matters rest with the conclusion that Frederick the Great, too, was a child of his times, but rather one must discover what degree of significance may be attached to his actions as opposed to those of fellow rulers. Measured by the standards of his own age, the "infamy" of the invasion of Silesia turns out to be minor. On the other hand, its political importance becomes all the more evident: it doubled the potential of Prussia, a pure warrior-state in the eyes of contemporaries. In comparison with this, of what moment were the larcenous wars of the "archmilitarist" Louis XIV, what actual effect did they have in percentage terms?

The net result of Ritter's investigation . . . is quite clear: in the eighteenth century when *raison d'état* was applied with strict logic to the army as the center of things, when both society and individual persons were shaped according to this model, when a policy of expansionism was systematically pursued on this basis, in short when militarism in the normal sense of the word reached its zenith — precisely at this juncture it is impossible to speak of the existence of militarism. This is a paradoxical outcome, but it has been achieved logically on the basis of a specific premise. Since in Ritter's view *raison d'état* and militarism are mutually exclusive by definition, since however a Prussian *raison d'état* unquestionably exists in light of the final military success, the presence of Prussian militarism must simply be denied. To be sure, in normal parlance militarism and *raison d'état* are by no means irreconcilable. Rather, there is such a thing as militaristic *raison d'état,* the product of the fusion of both concepts. And it was Prussia that made it a potent force in history.

WALTHER HUBATSCH (b. 1915) has worked in many different fields of modern European history. His view of Frederick as a unique amalgam of Enlightenment influences and Prussian tradition within the general framework of Absolutism presupposes the predominance of an abstract force, *raison d'état,* in political history. The complexity of his interpretation reflects the metaphysical orientation of one school of German historical thought. While based upon the results of more recent research, the analysis is hardly less conservative than Ritter's.*

Walther Hubatsch

A Variety of Enlightened Despotism

Frederick's most dramatic and most momentous actions have drawn the special attention of historians like a magnet, not only generally but also with regard to the formulation of what we may call the problem of *raison d'état.* Thus, his understanding of this crucial political principle is artificially assumed to stem from his young manhood, more precisely from 1740 when the twenty-eight-year-old monarch began to perform great deeds after a period of tranquil meditation. Very frequently—and not without some satisfaction—writers have pointed to the contrast between the governmental program announced in his *Antimachiavell* and the invasion of Silesia. There have been attempts to demonstrate the rebirth of Machiavelli in Frederick by means of strange, illogical historical associations. "In the sphere of foreign policy there is little difference between the two," so Gooch imagines that he must conclude.[1] How curious it is that this English scholar has already justified Machiavelli as a thoughtful patriot and is unwilling to accept the same excuse for Frederick! The fact of the matter is that there is a fundamental disparity between a theorist, whose existence one can tolerate without any noticeable ill effects, and an ambitious prince who destroys political equilibrium in the interest of his own state. Even if an

[1] Gooch, *Frederick the Great: the Ruler, the Writer, the Man,* p. 276.

*From Walther Hubatsch, *Das Problem der Staatsräson bei Freidrich dem Grossen* (Göttingen: Musterschmidt-Verlag, 1956), pp. 8–35. Translated by Thomas M. Barker. Some footnotes omitted.

eager reading of Machiavelli's theses did fail to make an impression upon Frederick (despite his determination to refute them), sixteenth-century concepts surely change their character completely after the passage of two hundred years, that is to say, once they have been removed from the living political context of the Italian *polis* and transformed into abstractions. Frederick did not have a true grasp of the reality of the Italian past any more than did any of the historians of his time. Thus *The Antimachiavell* can scarcely be said to be based upon tangible elements. Its author simply assumes that Machiavelli's propositions remain valid in the Age of Reason. Hence, when Frederick disproves them, his success is easy, in fact just as easy as it is later on for critics of Prussianism to claim victory at a cheap price. . . . Such a misunderstanding is possible only if Machiavelli's intellectual world is equated straightaway with the idea of *raison d'état*. In the meantime, however, research has opened the door to an understanding of certain factors of a traditional character operative in Prussian history. Taken together, they constitute a background hitherto largely ignored.[2]

It is significant that in *The Antimachiavell* Frederick is trying very hard to buttress his countertheses. As yet he did not have any concrete experiences of his own. He had to take refuge in reading materials and personal inspiration. Still, as an acute observer of current events, he did not neglect reality entirely. He did not sketch his contrasting picture on a utopian basis alone. He was able to stand on the foundation of inherited forms of

political life, a legacy with which he was personally well acquainted. Doubtlessly some of the maxims enunciated in *The Antimachiavell* derive from this source. For example, the postulate that princely power must serve the commonweal clearly reflects the older argument of common utility. Therefore we shall have to examine the genesis of Frederick's understanding of *raison d'état* on a dual basis. First, we must ask, to what extent was it determined by educational experience? Secondly, to what degree did it arise from actual experience? Once again, with reference to the controversial early period of Frederick's reign, experience can have but one meaning; namely, to study the origins of three particular components: tradition, assimilated knowledge, and living patterns.

Arnold Berney has shown in his valuable study of Frederick's education how the self-awareness of the young prince was accentuated by the French literature he so carefully selected for himself. Hence Frederick's development is a prime example of political self-education . . . No matter how correct this judgment may be, it still should not be accorded primary significance. Von Ranke was right in rejecting any attempt to "extract a common system of ideas from Frederick's literary works"[3] . . . Hartung arrives at the essence of the matter when he concludes that throughout his life Frederick was conservative in his choice of reading matter, in other words, he was hardly sympathetic to literary innovation.[4] Therefore reference solely to such theoretical writings must remain an inadequate device for understanding his political thinking. His actions as a ruler must be considered simultaneously. Likewise it is vain to

---

[2] Three recent works deserve special mention. They are: Erich Hassinger, "Das politische Testament Richelieus," *Historische Zeitschrift*, CLXXIII (1952), 485–503; Fritz Hartung, "Der aufgeklärte Absolutismus," *Historische Zeitschrift*, CLXXX (1955), 15–42; and Gerhard Oestreich, "Justus Lipsius als Theoretiker des neuzeitlichen Machtstaates," *Historische Zeitschrift*, CLXXXI (1956), 31–78.

[3] Leopold von Ranke, "Zwölf Bücher preussischer Geschichte," vol. 29, *Gesammelte Werke*, p. 292.

[4] Hartung, pp. 20, 30.

probe the whole corpus of his work in an effort to trace the momentary linguistic application of the phrase *raison d'état*. What evidence do we really have about the nature of *raison d'état* when we learn in the *Political Testament* of 1752 that this principle must be followed without prejudice and that the interest of the state must be the only guiding light in the counsels of the prince? Any more exact analysis of Frederick's writings will make it obvious that he is hardly original and that his dicta merit consideration more because of the weight of his royal position than on account of the autonomous character of his observations and rules. This must be made clear despite the admiration which Wilhelm Dilthey expressed for the latitude of Frederick's Enlightened ideals.[5] To be sure, the King is thoroughly permeated with rationalist thinking. He is a passionate adherent of the trends of his age although he is hardly the only eighteenth-century sovereign of whom this may be said. On the other hand, his wide-ranging political tracts present but a single facet of latter-day Absolutism, its theoretical aspect, that is. No matter how astonished we may be to note Frederick's refusal to be content with abstractions and to observe how he seeks to penetrate reality with his rules and insights, much of what he says remains schematic, a mere outline, an intrinsically utopian plan. Despite all the important written evidence, it is impossible to deal thoroughly and exhaustively with Frederick's concept of the state on a literary basis. Such an undertaking is more feasible if one considers his political testaments, the intimate character of which obviates the suspicion of their being addressed to a public whose applause the author expected.

The political testaments of the House of Hohenzollern, which extend from the time of the Great Elector to that of Frederick, may be linked both to the broader traditions of this genre of European princely literature and to the more limited heritage of the dynasty itself. They are rich in expressions of political principle and experience. On occasion the concept of *raison d'état* also appears. More significant is the fact that within the same family, throughout an uninterrupted sequence of generations and on the same political soil, one can ascertain the existence of an amazing continuity of viewpoints and given circumstances. Seen within the context of this legacy of political writing, Frederick's interpretation of *raison d'état* loses something of the character of an occasionally encountered maxim or of a fundamentally fresh revelation of knowledge. At the same time, however, there is a sharp distinction between the Hohenzollern and the French concepts of Absolutism. The idea of *raison d'état* did not originate in France. Rather, it developed there a peculiar profile of its own since it came to be associated most intimately with royal absolutism of the modern kind. In accordance with the guidelines of *raison*, Richelieu first had to establish internal order. (Admittedly, peace was precarious as became evident during the Fronde). Therefore domestic politics always had to be accorded preference. In Richelieu's France *raison d'état* was equivalent to sailing orders which would enable the ship of state to escape from chaotic, reef-strewn waters into the breadth and freedom that marked the open waters of great political possibilities. This was a frame of reference entirely foreign to Frederick. The status of political martial law, which ended France's chaotic civil strife, did not apply to Brandenburg-Prussia. The new monarch inherited a realm that was well governed internally. In such an environ-

---

[5] See Introduction, p. 3. — Ed.

ment *raison d'état* did not signify a harnessing of centrifugal energies but rather a concentration of resources in order to secure, perfect, and augment the influence of the state. The goal Frederick always had in mind, and sometimes even reached, was domestic development. Prosperity would guarantee the means for maintaining an army able to command respect and free the kingdom from the inhibiting effects of foreign subsidies, thereby assuring genuine sovereignty, a feeling of independence, and protection from the arbitrary behavior of one's neighbors. An eighteenth-century polity of this kind affords a "classic example of the primacy of foreign affairs."[6]

While even in Friderican Prussia the concept of *raison d'état* was not related exclusively to foreign policy, the latter was unquestionably predominant. This constitutes a rather novel situation if one considers Richelieu's ideas[7] and even more so if the comparison is made with older expressions of constitutional theory in Germany itself. Veit Ludwig von Seckendorff states in the introduction to his *Teutscher Fürstenstaat:* "Nevertheless, in using the word 'state,' I do not mean what is nowadays often understood thereby, for there is no kind of treachery, abomination, or frivolity which one does not seek to justify in certain, perverse quarters by referring to the 'state,' *'ratione status,'* or 'affairs of state.'"[8] This declaration represents not only a renunciation of Machiavellism. Its author also relates *raison d'état*, as he understands the phrase, to an ideal of just government or, if one substitutes modern terminology, to domestic policy. *Raison d'état,* as the

phrase was used in seventeenth-century German from Conring's[9] time, applies only to the territorial state and not to the Holy Roman Empire. Constitutional theory has likewise ceased to define the functions of the state on the basis of Biblical revelation and hence has rejected the wealth of experience contained in the Bible. The political doctrines of the small German territorial states of the later seventeenth and the eighteenth century thus rest upon secularized foundations. In addition to this change (which took place first) the evolution of a *raison d'état* specifically suited to the local principalities presupposes serious belief in the idea of sovereignty. For the period prior to 1648 such faith cannot be taken for granted.[10] However, from that date on there is an egotistical streak to the idea of *raison d'état* in Germany. It becomes most obvious in the larger territorial entities. The Wittelsbachs [Bavaria], the Hohenzollerns, the Wettiners [Saxony], and the Welfs [Hannover] unanimously refused to render services of vassalage to the House of Habsburg. Even within alliances the main objective was to make one's own resources more effective. "Alliances are good, but one's own strength is better," says the *Political Testament* of the Great Elector. Writing in 1768 and borrowing almost literally from this document, Frederick asserts that one must rely more on one's own strength than on the help of allies—a striking parallel of judgment and experience, to which others might be added. Therefore, to follow the traditions of the House

---

[6] Heinrich Heffter, "Vom Primat der Aussenpolitik," *Historische Zeitschrift,* CLXXI (1951), 4.
[7] Hassinger, p. 486.
[8] Veit Ludwig von Seckendorff, *Teutscher Fürstenstaat* (Frankfurt, 1656), "Vorrede."

[9] Hermann Conring (1606–1681) was founder of the science of statistics and likewise established German law as an autonomous discipline. He was also interested in political history, constitutional theory, medicine, and pharmacy.—Ed.
[10] The Peace of Westphalia accorded *de facto* sovereignty to the principalities of the Holy Roman Empire.—Ed.

of Brandenburg did not mean governing according to proven rules as much as it meant meeting the requirements of political situations by always showing the same kind of flexibility and by continually exploiting the full resources of the state.

Ever-increasing distrust in the permanency of political conditions went hand in hand with observance of perpetual change in the relationships between states. To quote from Frederick's *Political Testament* of 1768: "Who, for example, would have foreseen in 1670 that Russia could become a threat to all of Europe? Who would have thought in 1700 that Sweden would suffer humiliation? Who would have believed in 1712 that it would be possible for France to ally with the House of Austria, and Sweden with Russia? All these things have come to pass without their having been foreseen." Yet the conclusion drawn from this evidence was not resignation, the dominant attitude in Electoral Brandenburg before 1640,[11] but rather intensified activity. The admonition of the Great Elector never to sit still and the urgent advice of the restless Frederick William I to work hard and to handle all business one's self were words of wisdom heeded by Frederick II when he followed well-worn domestic trails and when he struck out upon new paths in foreign policy. Nevertheless, in Brandenburg military objectives were never permitted to become more important than the principle of maintaining the state. Political tradition was put to use according to rational standards, and so its long-range effect was to thwart ambition and expansionistic tendencies.

Within the same context it is necessary to refer to a trend in the development of cultural history . . . , more particularly to . . . Justus Lipsius, an arbitrary interpreter of Machiavelli who also resurrected Neostoicism. . . .[12] Hintze was the first to point out that modern *raison d'état* came to Brandenburg via Calvinism or by means of "the influence of the strictly ascetic forms of Protestantism taken as a whole."[13] In more recent times this conclusion has been amplified and explained with greater precision. One can demonstrate the existence of Neostoicism in Frederick even down to details. A case in point is skeptical judgment of fellow men: references to characteristics such as "malevolence" and "cunning" are just as common in Lipsius' writings as in his. Lipsius, too, mocked the belief in "children pure as the angels." It is possible to prove the existence of the moral problem of *raison d'état* and the solution of *prudentia mixta* not only in Lipsius' work but also in Frederick's political testaments. For, according to Lipsius, it is licit in the interests of the state to mingle deceit with political wisdom (which otherwise should be kept pure). Frederick, drawing upon experiences in the Seven Years' War, says the same thing in his *Political Testament* of 1768: "In my opinion one should wander from the straight and narrow path as little as possible. If one notices that another ruler is not behaving honorably, it is certainly

---

[11] Prior to the accession of the Great Elector (1640) Brandenburg was driven in various directions by the currents of the Thirty Years' War, being unable to offer effective resistance to whatever power was momentarily strongest. — Ed.

[12] The Dutch scholar Justus Lipsius (Joest Lips), 1547–1606, taught at German, Flemish, and Dutch universities and made great contributions to the study of the Latin classics, especially by editing and publishing the works of Seneca. The philosophical treatises of this first-century A.D. writer emphasize, *inter alia*, the need for righteous conduct, whereas his Greek-influenced tragedies stress the baseness of human behavior. See footnote 2.

[13] Otto Hintze, "Kalvinismus and Staatsräson in Brandenburg zu Beginn des siebzehnten Jahrhunderts," vol. 3, *Gesammelte Abhandlungen*, p. 290.

permissible to pay him with similar coin. There are also situations where breaking one's promises is excusable, namely, when the sufferings and well-being of the fatherland require it." However, Frederick regarded such tactics as "abominations." As late as 1752 he held that breach of treaty could be risked at the utmost only twice in a lifetime, and in 1755 he went so far as to establish no more than four presuppositions of extreme necessity which would justify such action. It is impossible to discern any direct influence of Machiavelli here. The arbitrariness of a capricious ruler has yielded to systematization of the prince's mode of behavior by means of a refined, multifaceted process of rationalization, to which even heads of state must be subject. This is a far cry from the Florentine's spiritual world. Seen in such a light, it is apparent that Neostoicism caused the idea of the absolutist state to undergo intellectual elaboration. Frederick, for his part, became acquainted with this new influence via the remarkable detour of the French *philosophes.*

Nonetheless, as Spranger has indicated, Frederick's "greatness of soul" was "more than ancient Stoicism." Such fortitude was "possible only in the modern era," for by then "Christian influences had so transformed the world that it was possible for a Protestant to live and work in it with an active faith, the origin of which he had almost forgotten." Yet Spranger went even further: "Frederick's free-ranging religious stance was possible only as an extreme form, an utmost extension of Protestantism. Its nucleus was firm belief and unqualified commitment to the virtues of conscience, deprived, albeit, of every trace of dogmatism. From time to time the King had words of praise for Luther. However, he would not have reckoned himself a member of the Grace-

oriented ecclesiastical structure erected by the great Reformer but only of the Church as an educational entity. And it is at this juncture that the Church ceases to be visible."[14] For our part we may add that it was not a completed historical process which placed Frederick within this Protestant developmental context but rather the practice of government. He accumulated a fund of empirical experience which complemented the peculiar traditions of his country.

Machiavellism of the Italian-French type was entirely alien to northern Germany. If the Protestant princes of the sixteenth and seventeenth centuries often said that they wished to lead a divinely blissful life characterized by peace and honor, the objective of their eighteenth-century descendents was not basically different save that peace had been transformed into indolence, divine bliss into the pleasures of the table, and honor into social gallantry. This was not Machiavellism by any stretch of the imagination, and Frederick's *Antimachiavell* was capable of earning the applause not only of the French *philosophes* but also of the German rationalists, including certain of the princes. Even if the Welfs, Wettiners, and Wittelsbachs pursued dynastic politics according to the Habsburg example, the fact *per se* is by no means evidence of genuine *raison d'état,* of a "law of momentum," to use Meinecke's phrase, inherent in their territories. Not even Prussia's acquisition of a royal crown (1701) was treated entirely in a dynastic sense. On the other hand, the Hohenzollern state *was* basically distinct from its surroundings in one respect. What differentiated it—and not merely

---

[14] Eduard Spranger, "Der Philosoph von Sanssouci," *Abhandlungen der preussischen Akademie der Wissenschaften,* philosopisch-historische Klasse, no. 5 (1942), p. 50.

from the eighteenth century on—from the customary forms of political life in Germany was the Calvinistic, Neostoical and, above all, ascetic cast of its government. A rationalization of the state's resources according to a *raison d'état* understood in this fashion had been pursued with baroque vigor ever since the time of the Great Elector. Already during his reign but even more obviously in the time of Frederick William I a religiously circumscribed form of life marked by moral rigor and simplicity was regarded as the basis of the prosperity of the House of Brandenburg. The credo of the more important Hohenzollerns was to seek nothing for one's self or for one's favorites but to put forth every possible exertion in the interest of a collectively and abstractly conceived state. It makes no difference whether this concept of a ruler's functions is called enlightened, creative, or benevolent despotism. And therefore only to a limited degree may we rank Frederick the Great among the Enlightened Despots—that is, if the Enlightenment is understood to mean independence from traditional circumstances. Despite the sharp contrast between the characters of Frederick and his father the royal *philosophe* could not and did not wish to carry out any plan for a fundamental renovation of the structure of state. Frederick William I's work was perpetuated in the bureaucratic machinery he created, in the corps of officials he employed, and in the political institutions he established. It is actually distressing to recall how during the disastrous period of the Seven Years' War Frederick's father appeared in the son's dreams—as De Catt informs us—and how Frederick frequently expressed the wish to justify himself before the spirit of his progenitor. Frederick says the same thing himself in his *Memorabilia of the House of Brandenburg*. We do not mean to suggest that this book provides evidence that *raison d'état* was dictated by family interests or by dynastic considerations. The royal historiographer was simply trying to teach himself something about the origins of his territory and its political problems. He realized that the state of the Great Elector and Frederick William I was a personal heritage. Thus we do not encounter any rationalistic airs but rather, as Ritter puts it, "a broad and extensive study of the past."[15] Could not Frederick's *raison d'état* also have been nourished from the reservoir of his ancestors' practical experience? When he was crown prince Frederick William I affixed the motto "not only for one's self" to his banners, whereas in 1740 young Frederick exploited what he considered a unique opportunity to enlarge his state. This juxtaposition of incidents from the careers of both men serves to illustrate a common quality of autonomous thinking with respect to the function of government and constitutes but one of many resemblances. The warning of the old Soldier King, deriving from a religiously grounded view of a ruler's responsibilities, not to wage any unjust wars corresponds to the pledge of a more mature Frederick not "to grab any more cats by the tail." In addition to older principles and the costly lesson learned in the school of personal experience the sage of Sans Souci also came to realize that an enlarged Prussia could maintain its place within the European political system only if it kept the peace and only if the balance among the great powers remained undisturbed. *Raison d'état* of seventeenth-century territorial origin thus merged, quite inevitably, with elements of a more sublime character.

---

[15] Ritter, *Frederick the Great*, p. 62.

The factors that permit us to deduce what may be called Friderican *raison d'état* therefore prove to be of highly diverse provenance. Frederick's theory of the state and the famous quotation about the prince being the first servant of the state are hardly inventions of his, as Hartung has shown. Frederick was sufficiently perspicacious to understand that a statesman cannot create opportunities but only exploit them, achieving "what is possible" [Bismarck]. Ritter emphasizes the rational limitations and the sobriety of Frederick's striving for power and agrees with Hintze, who regarded a moderate, pensive *raison d'état* as the filtering mechanism of the royal intellect.[16] According to Ritter reason of state is a coupling of practical comprehension of reality with ethical good sense. Hence Enlightened ideals do not necessarily clash with *raison d'état*, as Meinecke (who thought that he perceived two, contradictory tendencies in Frederick) maintained. For there is yet another, a third such tendency, which Meinecke preferred to ascribe to the Enlightenment but which must be considered an autonomous trait in view of our previous discussion of traditional features. We mean Frederick's concept of service. Fulfillment of duty and the ideal of hard work are not necessarily Enlightenment phenomena. Rather, they point backward to the earlier era of Protestant princely ethics when *raison d'état*, as it was first interpreted by German theorists, seemed to apply exclusively to domestic politics.

An effort to draw together the whole of the state in all of its parts and to frustrate special interests is detectable already in the case of the Great Elector and is even more evident, in a more modern way,

when we look at Frederick. The old principle that the common good outweighs private welfare and constant, painstaking care for the state as an integral reality are factors that ultimately condition statesmen to seek stability and permanency instead of "change and flux" (the motto of Gustavus Adolphus). This commitment to the task at hand is quite different from the absolute, secularized logic, the abstract maxims of *raison d'état* and guidance of the state in a strictly mathematical fashion which were to be found so perfectly developed in France. Without having had any such intention Frederick was responsible for the practical realization of a special kind of German absolutism. While this North German prince was perhaps Enlightened, he was by no means absolute according to the law, because the ideal of service and the awareness of a final reckoning—in short, the particular form of *raison d'état* operative within the context of local tradition—imposed certain conditions upon him. This was true not only for the person of the ruler. One must not forget that the monarch was simply the most distinguished servant of the state who presided over other active officials and military personnel. Certainly the individual bureaucrat did not develop any *raison d'état* of his own. Nevertheless, in Prussia he always helped to bear the responsibility for affairs of state. The numerically quite tiny but well-educated and enlightened officialdom of the eighteenth century possessed much more autonomy in administrative practice—the documents prove this—than the modern state would ever permit. Whoever consults the records and compares the situation in Brandenburg's army and state administration in the mid-seventeenth century with circumstances a hundred years later will

---

[16] Hintze, *loc. cit.*, p. 481.

et a vivid impression of the educational accomplishments of the Hohenzollern rulers. What refinement of the concept of honor and service was necessary before the typical figure of the Prussian officer and bureaucrat could be formed—a kind of individual whom one could consider a paragon of faithfulness to duty and of reliability within a society which was still very corrupt!

To be sure, any exposition of the origins of Frederick's political ideas is insufficient by itself to prove that not only in domestic affairs was there a resolution of Meinecke's problem of the conflict of *Ethos* and *Kratos* but that in foreign relations, too, *raison d'état* meant more than a brutal drive for power. Frederick's own pronouncements, especially in the political testaments (which must be regarded as intimate revelations, even as state secrets) seem to confirm the opinion of those who claim to see in the royal *philosophe* if not a cynic at least a realist whose behavior knew no moral scruples. "Always remember," says the *Political Testament* of 1768, "that every great ruler desires to extend his dominion . . . *Raison d'état* requires that these intentions remain covered by impenetrable veils and that one postpone their execution as long as one lacks the means to do so successfully. One must pursue the interest of the state blindly and ally with that power whose momentary interests best comport with one's own." Hence Meinecke spoke of the "Enlightenment ideal in conflict with the demon of *raison d'état*." He saw in *raison d'état* "the inevitability of political action." Ritter protested passionately against this determinism. Stephen Skalweit also stressed that "obedience to the dictates of *raison d'état* never led to the extinction of humane attitudes in Frederick's political

thought."[17] Indeed, how could this have been the case if we understand reason of state to mean not a demonic, aggressive force but an element that operates in a cautious, pensive fashion and acts as a brake? Power may not be equated with compulsion. The demon was fettered. This fact is not obvious, especially since barbarism was part of the eighteenth-century way of life even when it was supposed to have a disciplinary purpose. For example, let us compare the penal code of the British Navy with Prussian political practices. Even as early as the Silesian wars Frederick was so habituated to the exercise of restraint that he subjected all his actions to higher principles of state. If one discounts personal ambition, his policy in 1740 was less determined by *raison d'état* than by dynastic power interests identical to those of other princely houses of the day.

At the same time another factor, more indicative of the future, impinges quite noticeably; namely, the ideal image of the Enlightened ruler. Frederick tried to conform to an archetypical pattern by means of education and meditation. His efforts found their first, sketchy expression in *The Antimachiavell*. Nor must one forget how well his career accorded with Prussian tradition. The initial harmony was based on the momentary domestic circumstances of the state. Later on it was due to historiographical activity in which the royal scholar sought to appropriate for himself the past developmental trends of his country. Towering above everything else and an element that became increasingly important in determining his capacity for work was the aging king's

---

[17] Stephan Skalweit, "Das Problem von Recht und Macht und das historiographische Bild Friedrichs des Grossen," *Geschichte in Wissenschaft und Unterricht* II (1951), p. 103.

ideal of service, hardened by the dire necessities of war and applied relentlessly to the job of reconstruction.

Such considerations leave us with a final objection to consider in our attempt —successful up to now, we trust—to regard Friderican *raison d'état* impartially. One should not assume that this concept has the same meaning for Frederick the Crown Prince, as for Frederick the architect of the Princes' League. Experience and tradition enable a person to perceive change and make distinctions, and thus when Frederick's political theory is submitted to analysis, some differentiation is necessary.

One can summarize the problem of *raison d'état* as it relates to Frederick the Great in the following manner. Since Meinecke's pioneering exercise in intellectual history, younger scholars have been able to contribute a series of new and varied observations which supplement the earlier picture. As the task of interpretation is carried forward the still somewhat imprecise concept of *raison d'état* will require sharper focus so that there may be a more exact delimitation of the successive phases that characterize Frederick's views about the nature of the state. The undeniable educational influence of the Enlightenment upon royal political thinking provides only an approximate point of departure for the evolution from a dynastic mentality to a more august, abstract notion of the state. While Frederick's crucial significance in the victory of the principle of *raison d'état* may be said to stem from this transformation, the process itself will be better understood by studying the actual practice of government rather than by any theoretical discussion. Experience based upon the traditions of the House of Hohenzollern is no less important as a source of Frederick's concept of the state

than educational experience. He is linke more closely than has been previousl assumed to the continuum of Brander burg's political heritage. This is th factor that differentiates conditions i Prussia from both the French version (*raison d'état* and the legacy of Germa political thinking with its eighteenth century aftereffects. At the same time is clear that the intellectual currents (Neostoicism and Calvinism helped t strengthen indigenous patterns. If w tie these diverse roots together, what w have is a maxim in Kant's sense of th word [that is, a set of circumstances tha produce a specific result]. The monarch highly personalized ideal of service repre sents its zenith, whereas *raison d'éta* finds concrete expression in the everyda operation of the elements it encompasse

On the basis of what we have been abl to establish up to this point, we may . . [raise] the question of the degree to whicl Frederick was an influence in the devel opment of German political behavio Meinecke was quite correct in his las book, *The German Catastrophe*, when h cautioned against mindless Borussianism Rather, our present task is to try to dis cern beginnings and motivational force in Prussian history and to relate then on a different plane to German an European history. All the same, th historical effect of a figure such as Freder ick should not be overestimated, despit respect for his greatness. Richelieu's shad ow, which lay for centuries over th border of the Rhine, has little in commor with the French statesman's real profile But should a historian give way to resig nation in face of the observation tha artificial historical images can effect th public mind more potently than actua events? In its description of the eigh teenth century the otherwise so excellen French *Clio* series states, "Frederick I aved the road that links Luther to Bismarck and Hitler."[18] This view not only presupposes highly schematic causal relationships in the self-developing historical process. It is also unhistorical because it fails to account for external influences. It is not even correct with regard to what the principle of *raison d'état* teaches us in this connection. Possibly, among the various interpretations to which we have referred, there is some minor, hidden link between the Prussian monarch and Protestantism, but there is surely no path to Bismarck and even less so to Hitler. The parallel of autocracy—inaccurate even in Bismarck's case—is psychologically enticing but historically imprecise since the presuppositions for applying the notion of *raison d'état* to the events of the nineteenth and twentieth centuries are quite different from those operative during Frederick's lifetime. This holds true not only for ruling personalities but also for social conditions and the make-up of the governing strata. In the eighteenth century there was only one segment of society that was concerned with the functioning of the state, namely, the landowners and the higher government officials. To this extent it is possible to label the Friderican state "aristocratic," assuming that one does not associate the term with the idea of a noble oligarchy such as existed in contemporary Sweden and Poland but merely wishes to establish a presupposition for Frederick's monarchical form of political leadership. To be sure, social divisions in Prussia were not basically different from those in Saxony, Bavaria, Austria, Poland, and—as far as the governing caste is concerned—in Russia too. To whatever degree there were differences, they lay in the varying abilities of these states to concentrate their political forces. It may be noted that in a chronological sense Prussia stood in the middle, between the analogous endeavors of Peter the Great and Joseph II. By no means did Brandenburg-Prussia make use of illicit military methods in the process. Indeed, for comparison's sake, let us recall how Saxony won the Polish crown the second time. It was by force of arms. Yet nowadays nobody would consider this fact sensational, and quite properly so.

Although we wish to limit ourselves to judging Frederick by the example of contemporaries, we cannot ignore the figure of Louis XIV. When we consider his career, it is clear that the nineteenth-century slogan of "militarism" used for Prussia must also apply to a whole epoch. Yet it would demonstrate remarkably little knowledge of the seventeenth and eighteenth centuries if one were to call the Great Elector, Frederick William I, and Frederick the Great all militarists. The formula of continuous militaristic expansion would restrict the history of Brandenburg-Prussia to an impermissible degree. There is, after all, a difference whether the army is the "center" (as Dehio cautiously expresses himself) of all political affairs or whether it is the yardstick by which they are measured. Nor is it any more feasible to place Frederick on the same level as Charles XII, whom, incidentally, the Prussian king appraises far more severely than does Voltaire.[19] The year 1740 did not establish a pattern in Prussia, whereas the Swedish monarch knew no form of "political leadership" other than resort to arms. If Prussia had really been concerned only with the exploitation of European power vacuums, many a favor-

---

[18] Series "Clio," *Le XVIIIe siècle* (Paris, 1952), p. 158.

[19] Both Frederick and Voltaire wrote about Charles' career. — Ed.

able moment would have presented itself after 1763. Therefore any firm equation of Charles XII with Frederick the Great — the Swedish ruler simply falls into the category of failures, losers, and the politically outmaneuvered — surely departs from historical reality. Frederick's historical greatness stands in sharp contrast to Charles XII, for it derives not only from his military deeds but also from his statesmanly achievements in both domestic and foreign affairs and from the fact that he symbolizes an epoch in European civilization. Did Charles ever win a province by making the best of a dangerous diplomatic situation? What symphonies did he compose, what poems and historical works did he write? He certainly had sufficient leisure for such things while he was imprisoned in Turkey. Surely a bold, initial success — the one feature common to both men — should not be considered a decisive factor. Rather, one must evaluate a person's lifework. Frederick's skill in practising the art of state is not evinced by the unrepeatable feats of 1740 but by his commitment to moderation. (Whether his reasons were ultilitarian or rational, ethical or dictated by fear, is irrelevant for the moment). He must therefore be ranked alongside Bismarck rather than the autocrats Napoleon and Hitler, who fell victim to Caesarism. The recent effort to prove the existence of a diagonal line between Frederick the Great and Hitler as a possible historical trend contradicts the actual course of events and the evidence of the sources to such an extent that it is simply impossible to accord with it.

Let us look at things for a moment with the eyes of contemporaries and compare Frederick the Great and Joseph II. Perhaps the special character of the Prussian king's *raison d'état* will then become more obvious. Although the Hohenzollern may have been in perfect harmony with the traditions of his state, we can in no way say the same of the Habsburg. The "law of momentum," to use Meinecke's description of *raison d'état*, in the Habsburg lands was not centralization. Indeed, the initial effect of Joseph's reforms was to evoke strong regionalism as a countervailing force. Joseph's admiration for Frederick may have caused him to regard his Prussian colleague as as Enlightened statesman, but he was mistaken. The Prussian machinery of state which Maria Theresa's son wished to copy was simply the further extension of a long reorganized and rationalized political entity based upon a population well disciplined in such forms of communal existence. The distinction between Joseph and Frederick is also evident when one considers ultimate results. Whereas Austrian liberalism developed into "Josephinism" at the beginning of the nineteenth century in order to contend with the growing nationality problem, there was no such thing as "Fridericanism" in Prussian Germany.

In this context we have also come to touch upon the question of Frederick's influence upon our own times, an issue often raised unhistorically and hence incorrectly. It is said with remarkable *sangfroid* that Frederick's deeds contributed to the sad occurrences of the twentieth century, just as if the Prussian king deliberately prepared the way for the coming of Bismarck and Hitler. We must differentiate sharply here. Frederick's life transpired in a present that belonged to him alone. He drew independently upon tradition after having taken his own environment into account. The purpose of his *raison d'état* was to acquire for Prussia a significant place among the great powers with as little risk as posible. He wanted to guarantee this position and make his country not merely tolerated but respected as well. The most that he could hope for was to lay the foundations upon which a successor could pursue his duties as a ruler in keeping with the tasks imposed by a new and different present. We know how vain even this modest expectation was. Twenty years after his death his edifice of state lay in ruins. The Prussian reformers, who themselves stemmed for the most part from Frederick's traditions, did not attempt to reconstruct it. Of course, even here we may discern some continuity (although the influence of the French Revolution surely extended to the Reform Edicts). In this regard it is possible to speak of a connection between Frederick the Great and Bismarck, for the political thinking of both men had to be concerned with the same country, the same presuppositions and neighbors. Nevertheless, there is no direct "line that reaches from Frederick to Bismarck." Any attempt to make Frederick responsible for the deeds of nineteenth-century Prussian politicians is sheer unhistorical reasoning. Such a thesis posits the existence of impotent Epigones who remain the captives of great personalities of the past. Full responsibility for success and failure must always rest in the hands of those who live in the present. It would be more appropriate to ask how Frederick's image, whether artificial or genuine, affected Bismarck's mind. Surely, the ideal of service, the feeling of responsibility for the state and devotion to work are to be found in both Bismarck and Frederick the Great. Yet did Bismarck require Frederick's example for these characteristics? Whether the eighteenth-century notion of *raison d'état*, difficult to define even in Frederick's case, determined Bismarck's behavior seems highly

questionable, quite apart from the fact that he was no sovereign. Hence, it is necessary to examine the thesis of Frederick's lasting influence separately in each case that may arise.

It is strange that since the end of the nineteenth century no new evidence has been presented to prove inexcusable behavior by Frederick. Thus current discussion of the issue takes place on the basis of a critical outlook entirely inappropriate to the world of the present. What may have made sense as an antidote to the Borussian legend is pointless nowadays. Slogans about Prussian hostility to the Empire and Prussian wars of conquest coined with reference to the events of 1866 were transferred to Frederick the Great in order to provide an argument for the continuity of evil features in this state.[20] These are seductive doctrines that can be used in a great variety of ways to whip up political passions. No European state has been spared of them. Yet they can never lead to a comprehension of historical reality. We must remember that prior to 1740 Prussia did not gain a single sliver of territory within the Empire either by conquest or by any other extralegal means. Brandenburg's fidelity to the Imperial House was legendary and often contrary to its own interests. Even in 1740 Frederick did not endanger the Empire even remotely as much as did Max Emmanuel of Bavaria at the beginning of the War of the Spanish Succession. It will be recalled that this Wittelsbach ruler, in conjunction with his relative, the Archbishop-Elector of Cologne, opened the Rhine passages to the French and permitted them to use Bavarian territory for their drive deep into southern Germany. This behavior, so

---

[20] The reference is to Klopp. See Introduction, p. 2.

obviously hostile to the Empire, has been forgotten. Despite the "antiemperor" Charles VII,[21] it has not been regarded as a "lasting trend." This is quite as it should be. But why deny Frederick the same historical understanding for his behavior in 1740? The basic reason for his decision to attack, namely, the challenge to Maria Theresa's accession posed by Saxony, Bavaria, and France, is not generally known. Fortunately, however, it is generally recognized that in 1756 Prussia did not run amok. Frederick was admittedly no more than a coparticipant in a world-wide colonial struggle (without of course any prospect of conquest or gain overseas) which had already begun and for which a military precondition, the enmity between British-ruled Hannover and France, existed in Central Europe even without Prussian involvement.

We have good reason for gradually turning our backs on nineteenth-century controversies and letting the historical facts of the eighteenth century speak for themselves. We need not undertake the fruitless effort of trying to alter them after they have occurred. While the intention of the present essay has been to direct attention to historical associations which lie outside long-established viewpoints, the underlying purpose was not to search for theoretical and abstract tendencies in Frederick's political thought but to illustrate how his views and experiences are interwoven with the structure and traditions of the Prussian state. Being a premise from which inferences are drawn, reason of state as applied to Frederick the Great has always presented the historian with a problem.

It cannot be described easily because is not something that is obvious an measurable. Perhaps one may define as a ceaseless striving for a supreme idea in affairs of state. Frederick's motivation become quite evident in his daily roun of service but even more so in the entice ments and perils to which his own prin ciples expose him. The concept of *raiso d'état* in Brandenburg-Prussia must al ways be understood only in terms of it momentary employment. To carry ou such an analysis in greater detail usin the rich source materials would be equiva lent to writing a history of this countr from the viewpoint of statesmanly re sponsibility. We have wished to do noth ing more here than to pose questions an to present some observations based upo many years' work with the sources. Fred erick of Prussia was not a personality wh enjoyed full freedom of decision, as hi 1740 error indicates. He did not exercis enduring historical influence in the wa glorifying, hero-worshipping writers o less distinguished, succeeding generation have sought to maintain. Nor was he a individual entirely subject to his environ ment, to the currents of his age, or t any dogmatic historical law such as th belief that men have to keep pace wit ineluctible trends in economic develop ment. Rather, Frederick was simply abl to stamp a personal note upon his era an the state he ruled. On the other hand, th historic personality of this Enlightene prince stands at the very end of an epoch Frederick's death and the outbreak of th French Revolution, which occurred with in five years of each other, mark the con clusion of this period in Europea history. In Frederick the Great we se incorporated for the last time both th theoretical and factual aspects of Absolut ism, accompanied by a refined expres sion of *raison d'état.*

---

[21] The Wittelsbach opponent of Maria Theresa who briefly wore the imperial crown. In Medieval times a *Gegenkaiser* was generally a creature of the opposition to a reigning emperor. — Ed.

HANS ROSENBERG (b. 1904), an *émigré* from Hitler's
Germany, has taught at Brooklyn College and
Berkeley. His career has been marked by many
important academic distinctions. Rosenberg's outline
of the growth of an ultimately ruinous bureaucratic
caste is a highly creative scholarly contribution. He
feels that the Prussian phenomenon should be
compared with parallel developments elsewhere.
The book from which the following excerpt on the
Friderican period is taken was first published as a
Harvard Historical Monograph.* He has also published
works on nineteenth-century political propaganda and
on economic history.

Hans Rosenberg

The Bureaucratic Class
and the Military State

Frederick II succeeded in retarding the
rise of aristocratic-bureaucratic absolutism in Prussia, but he was unable to
prevent it. Indeed, paradoxically enough,
he also did much to further it. He labored
hard to tighten up the working alliance
between the autocracy and the nobility.
For this alliance he paid a heavy price:
limitation of class competition in dynastic
employment; the stiffening of the noble
monopoly of the purchase and sale of
Rittergüter [knightly estates]; the extension of noble privileges in law and in
fact; the broadening of differences in the
treatment of nobles and nonnobles inside
and outside government service; the

reaffirmation of the superiority of inherited social rank over specialized
knowledge, practical experience, and
professional achievement; and the adop-
tion of a narrow policy of ennoblement.

The concomitant transformation of the
bureaucratic nobility was but another
phase of the new course. Its personnel
now became more fully representative
of the rival subgroups of the Prussian
nobility. Frederick II effected a very
significant reshuffling of the bureaucratic
top stratum by replenishing its member-
ship with men from entrenched family
dynasties of noble career bureaucrats,
and also with "outsiders." The latter were

* Reprinted by permission of the publishers from Hans Rosenberg, *Bureaucracy, Aristocracy and Autoc-*
racy: The Prussian Experience, 1660–1815. Cambridge, Mass.: Harvard University Press, Copyright, 1958,
by the President and Fellows of Harvard College. Pp. 155–174. Extensive footnotes omitted. This book is also
available as a Beacon paperback.

noble army officers and *Landrat*-squires[1] who were chosen because they were military service nobles and particularly distinguished landed nobles.

An extraordinarily astute, vigilant, and increasingly cynical statesman like *Fredericus rex* had considered reasons for detaching himself from his father's social policy. It was not simply personal fancy that induced him to threaten his own *Fiskale* [treasury officials] with death on the gallows, if they continued to inconvenience noble estate owners by reclaiming crown lands once "alienated" to them. Nor did Frederick drift thoughtlessly, when he made it almost impossible for a "gentilhomme" to be responsible to a "bourgeois" where positions of consequence in the state were concerned. In a system of personalized autocracy, the social prejudices, beliefs, and illusions of the supreme leader were quite important, especially when they were in harmony with the cardinal wishes and primary interests of the dominant social forces.

Whatever the significance of his celebrated literary devotion to some of the ideals of the Enlightenment, in his early years as Prussian king Frederick II acted like a recklessly ambitious political gambler. Bent on the pursuit of a foreign policy of strength with provocation, aggressive war, conquest by force, and personal glory, he firmly resolved to lift up his state to the rank of an admired and feared Great Power.

In order to become "the Great," Frederick needed a unified, socially cohesive, and pacified home front. To his way of thinking, the task of tightening his grip on men through guile and management, of making the Prussian people serve his ends, and of fostering both the fact and the

sense of common statehood called for closer bonds of union between the autocrat and the "active citizens," that is, the First Estate. Frederick, keenly sensitive to his historic, aristocratic heritage, was inclined to use the words "nobility" and "nation" synonymously for most practical purposes, for he regarded "la fleur de la noblesse" as "l'élite de la nation."

His policy of keeping down "the non-noble riff-raff" and of sustaining the nobility was the cornerstone of an all-pervasive sociopolitical pattern. His social policy widened the gulf between the governing classes and the governed masses. The political order was to be stabilized by freezing the old social system with its inequality of rights and opportunities and its castelike division of labor between nobles, burghers, and peasants.

Frederick's domestic policy retarded the interclass mobility so typical of the regime of his father and deliberately reverted to the ancient equation of gentle birth with "merit." Frederick preferred to assign an exalted political function to the nobility. He protected its class monopoly over large-scale private landowner-ship and agricultural credit, and he fortified its exclusive social position. He intensified the interaction and interpenetration of the military-bureaucratic institutions of the absolute monarchy and of the no less despotic "home rule" institutions, which sustained the traditional way of life of the squirearchy. He did his utmost to indoctrinate "the foremost and most brilliant estate of the state" with what he termed *esprit de corps et de nation*.

Through the dual policy of promoting the cooperation and interfusion of the governing elites on the one hand and of cunningly exploiting their rivalries on the other, he sought to overcome the most vulnerable feature of the Prussian

---

[1] *Landrat* = district magistrate. — Ed.

polity: its inherent, long-standing dualism. He did much for the nobility, because he expected it to do a great deal for him. And he attached such high hopes to the wellborn as "the foundation and the pillars of the state," because, in his estimation, the simple "von," if acquired by birth and underpinned by the ownership of land and inherited mastery over men, made all the difference in the world.

Frederick's whole conception of the state was rooted in the aristocratic way of thinking, which took for granted a society made up of groups of men of intrinsically different value. Hence he assumed that the middle classes could be animated only by base motives. To appoint men of such background, immutable endowment, and moral defectiveness to positions of trust in the government services was "the first step toward the decline and fall of the army" and thus of the authoritarian state itself. At best, their employment was a necessary evil. Hence, for instance, the promotion of numerous commoners to commissioned rank in the Prussian army during the Seven Years' War and the dismissal or demotion to inferior service functions of most of them after the return to peace.

To Frederick it was self-evident that only the wellborn and particularly the scions of old landed families could be ideal servants of his state. For he attributed to this category of men certain superior, ingrained qualities which justified their privileges and made them singularly fit to function as efficient and reliable manufacturers of obedience from below. They alone were capable of cultivating loyalties and ambitions of a lofty kind, of developing a *point d'honneur,* a longing for glory and the martial virtues and ideals, a disciplined passion for service as conveyors of despotic power from above to below, thus linking the majestic

autocrat at the top to the shapeless rabble at the bottom. They alone were born to lead a "heroic" life, to act with valor, fortitude, and inner zeal, ready, if not eager to make the supreme sacrifice for the sake of victory in battle. They alone, through education and indoctrination, through soft words and harsh threats, through rewards and punishment, could be induced to embrace "the Prussian Spirit" and to identify themselves as a matter of self-interest with the monarchical state and its expansion. They alone had the moral stamina needed for the development of an habitual sense of obligation and an active sentiment of attachment to an idea. They alone were justified in adhering to an exalted conception of their dignity, rank, and mission. They alone had a natural claim to social superiority and political precedence in the dynastic state, for only they could be expected to equate class honor with national honor.

These few, then, had come into the world to command and to lead the many under the watchful eye of "the first servant of my state." The power of the state had to be restricted caste power. This was the essence of Frederick's aristocratic-militarist ideology of *esprit de corps et de nation.* In his state even the sentiments of "Prussian nationalism" were to be a social function of special privilege, fit for noblemen only. Consequently, in exchange for their political submission, the higher public dignities should be the exclusive domain of honorific noble class employment. In this vital matter, a royal drill sergeant like Frederick William I revealed more liberality of outlook and freedom from prejudice than his brilliantly gifted, enlightened son, the captive of class bias and aristocratic superstitions.

Montesquieu's fundamental maxim "no

monarch, no nobility; no nobility, no monarch" was destined to have quite a career in Prussia under Frederick II, who did much to stabilize the absolute monarchy by converting it into an aristocratic oligarchy headed by the heirs of noble privilege, thus shaping the pattern of the personnel administration of the Great Frederick.

Frederick II could not halt, let alone reverse the trend which under his predecessor had given the lion's share of the administrative councilorships to commoners. To be sure, there were repeated royal directives requesting that "vacancies in the provincial boards should be filled with noblemen to a larger extent than heretofore." Implementation, however, was difficult, especially before the end of the Seven Years' War.

Professionally qualified noble candidates were in short supply. Frederick cordially welcomed nobles of foreign extraction in his army, but he regarded them as "undesirable" in the civil state service. He was afraid that for most of these gentlemen *travailler pour le Roi de Prusse* would be nothing but a steppingstone; later they might sell their acquired "Prussian skills" to foreign governments. Besides, Frederick had learned through hard experience that technical experts taken from the middle classes were "used to work more assiduously and to go more fully into details" than their noble colleagues. But he also believed that noblemen, especially if they were "tall and had brains," would do better in the army. Finally, the logic of growing "bureaucratization" and the continued drive for the improvement of efficiency, combined with the unplanned, stubborn facts of social mobility, proved strong enough in real life to prevent the hierarchy of hereditary estates and royal wishful thinking from blocking the social ascent of commoners and the downgrading of a sizable section of the nobility. Many of the nominating top officials, increasingly concerned with raising the standards of admission and promotion, recommended commoners rather than titled aristocrats for appointment in the higher grades.

In consequence, the numerical ratio between the two elements did not significantly change in the administrative bureaucracy during the reign of Frederick II. As a matter of fact, the preponderance of *roturiers*[2] in the upper brackets grew. After Cocceji's personnel reforms, the vast majority of the councilorships in the judicial bureaucracy, too, was gradually captured by nonnobles. The imposition of more exacting entrance requirements and working standards crowded out many noble job candidates, actual and potential. Furthermore, army service had grown in popularity in noble circles, and the *Regierungen* [local government units] had lost much of their original attractiveness as exclusive bastions of Junker strength.

Oddly enough, it was only after Frederick's death that the numerical balance between nobles and commoners began to change seriously to the detriment of the "nonnoble riff-raff." This innovation gained some momentum in the age of the French Revolution, when the sponsors of the Prussian Legal Code of 1794 "improved" the merit system by setting aside, as a matter of right, all state dignities of significance for members of the nobility. However, this belated legal victory of "the noble reaction" was, in part, offset by liberalizing the royal policy of ennoblement. Illegitimate sons of wellborn army officers and distinguished members

---

[2] Non-nobles.—Ed.

of the upper civil bureaucracy, held down by Frederick II, now entered the ranks of the nobility. They were joined by wealthy merchants and manufacturers like Treskow and Eckardstein, heralding the feeble beginning of the social recognition of a new pioneering business elite. Nevertheless, the recently ennobled Minister von Struensee, a former high school teacher, exaggerated when he told the French *chargé d'affaires* in 1799: "The salutary revolution which you have made from below will come about gradually in Prussia from above. The King is a democrat in his own way. He works unceasingly on plans for the limitation of the privileges of the nobility and will follow the scheme of Joseph II but with slower methods. In a few years there will be no longer any privileged class in Prussia."

Frederick II concentrated his efforts at reform in personnel selection upon the crucial group, the bureaucratic nobility. He proceeded with caution and with moderation. Handicapped by the great scarcity of "good noblemen," who were intelligent, skilled, and experienced enough to replace, without causing administrative anarchy, the nonnoble councilors, Frederick, of necessity, had to content himself with sifting the "very important persons" only.

The remaking of the bureaucratic nobility entailed restaffing and internal regrouping. Royal intervention fostered, by design, the resurrection of the old landed nobility of birth, largely reoriented through army service, as the possessor of executive top power, though now under the crown and, therefore, surrounded by a capricious and hazardous network of checks and balances.

Frederick did not disrupt administrative power by dismissing the nobles of ascent from the service. He kept the newly ennobled in office until they died or grew very old and lost their usefulness. He actively supported the outstanding representatives of this group, Cocceji and Boden, against the machinations of their highborn colleagues. In grudging recognition of the fact that "unfortunately at the present time really capable noblemen for such a position" were not forthcoming, Frederick even promoted a handful of nonnoble career men to leading posts in the service. But such was the rigidity of his policy of social discrimination that he denied these men elevation to noble rank. In official status, as recognized by Frederick, they were the professional, but not the social equals of the members of the purified bureaucratic nobility.

A few isolated members of the "illborn" found a little backdoor of hope. Thus Domhardt after endless waiting and tireless campaigning gained admission. Domhardt was an administrator of eminent quality, who had been a large farmer and laid the foundation of his fortune as a horse trader. He achieved the signal triumph of being appointed to the unique position of president of the two provinces East and West Prussia, of becoming one of the largest and most enterprising landowners in the kingdom, and even of wheedling a patent of nobility out of his royal master. As a rule, Frederick II reserved this rare honor for men who had distinguished themselves in military service. Among the twenty ministers whom he appointed to the General Directory from 1740 to 1786, there was only a single commoner, the lonely Friedrich Gottlieb Michaelis, a pharmacist's son, who reached the pinnacle of his bureaucratic career by being employed, though for two years only, as postmaster general, in professional and social prestige the least distinguished ministerial position in the service. The very rarity of these appointments merely confirmed the governing principle of cutting off administrative experts of defective social origin from the chance of competing for the highest dignities and most lucrative emoluments.

From the beginning of his political stewardship Frederick II left the old guard bureaucrats a little breathless and perturbed by filling important vacancies and newly created top posts almost exclusively with landed nobles of old lineage or with noble army officers on the active list, who were complete newcomers to the game and who assumed high service rank at one bound. With the aid of the considerate sovereign, the Junkers moved back to their ancient position of assured predominance in public administration. Thus the partially dispossessed began to dispossess their parvenu-dispossessors.

The nobility's continued decline in relative numbers within the administrative and judicial bureaucracies as a whole was more than counterbalanced by the fact that after 1740 almost all places of real profit, distinction, and decisive influence were reserved to members of the old nobility of descent. Under royal auspices they were reconstituted as a particularly privileged group. These select men were entrusted with the responsibility of presiding over the hierarchy of service officers and of managing through them the vast centralized domain of civil affairs. They were vested with the power to recommend appointments, promotions, bonuses, penalties, and dismissals, and to enforce the disciplinary codes. Not only did they have a firm grip on the execution of policy, as consultants they shared in its preparation. They were given a limited opportunity for making managerial decisions and for thinking out policy. The inferior task of trans-

forming royal orders and directives into red tape, of conducting minor investigations, and of supervising the clerical workers and petty field agents was left, in the main, to the councilors.

The nobility's job and power monopolies in the civil state included the diplomatic posts and the positions at the royal court and, consequently, a substantial portion of public income and dignities. Of far greater weight, in view of its political impact and its consequences for the rural and urban classes, was the fact that until 1806, save for a very few social climbers, all the newly appointed ministers forming the central executive authority, all the presidents of the provincial administrative and judicial boards, and all the *Landräte* came from well-established, though not necessarily old, noble families—as was demonstrated by the Danckelmanns and by von Jariges, Cocceji's successor. Noble birth, especially with wealth and influence to back it, was sufficient to dispense with the plebeian norm of examinations, "mandatory" since 1770, and with seniority. Von Münchow, for instance, was made minister for Silesia at the age of thirty-three; the able von Schlabrendorff at thirty-five; the unscrupulous Count von Hoym at thirty. Count von Finckenstein was twenty-one years of age when he became ambassador in Stockholm. Fourteen years later he was a minister of state.

Frederick's policy proved particularly profitable to those fierce and ungovernable families who hitherto had resisted active collaboration with "Hohenzollern despotism" and "Prussian collectivism." Frederick William I had felt greatly annoyed by these "spiteful and disobedient people" and resentfully singled out the Alvenslebens, Bismarcks, Schulenburgs as "the most prominent and the most adamant families" of the Old Mark.

Many English cavaliers who had supported the Stuart dynasty suddenly found themselves, after the "Glorious Revolution," on the side of "civil and religious liberty"; conversely, in Prussia, a score of Junker clans, encouraged by the re-ascendancy of the old nobility, discovered on which side their bread was buttered. At long last they fell into line, shed the spirit of rugged local independence and individual liberty and made their ancestral sense of social superiority serviceable to the cause of "noble reaction." By mending their fences, they found fat livings, although sometimes they had to be educated in their unfamiliar new duties by former *roturiers*. Thus, Cocceji, for example, received instructions from Frederick II to "break in" President Levin Friedrich von Bismarck, whose ideas His Majesty had found "at times very stupid."

A brilliantly successful representative of this group of belated proselytes was Schulenburg-Kehnert, for thirty-two years a Prussian minister and only twenty-nine when he attained that lofty rank. His vanity and greed were not satiated until he had snatched up the largest number of high-rating offices and sinecures in the civil administration ever held by a Prussian bureaucrat of the eighteenth century. At the same time, his thirst for the external paraphernalia of power and prestige also carried him far in the military hierarchy. "Because he had once served as a lieutenant," he deemed himself good enough, as Hermann von Boyen put it, to get himself gradually promoted to the rank of full general of the cavalry. Professionally, a dull though diligent man of routine and, personally, a pompous character, Schulenburg managed to keep alive, for his own benefit as well as for the sake of some of his fellows, the essentials of the old spoils system.

Other ministers like von Heinitz, von Schrötter, von Stein, wellborn and equipped with the necessary connections, also had not been asked to put themselves to the trouble of taking an examination when they entered the administrative aristocracy. But unlike Schulenburg, they were not only imaginative and forceful organizers, but also high-spirited men. Happily enough, a conceited mercenary like Schulenburg was but one among several distinctive types of noble top bureaucrats. As such, he made it crystal clear that not even the most generous material awards and social honors accorded for "meritorious service" were always sufficient to produce real loyalty to "Prussia" and to buy "patriotism." During the cataclysm of 1806 Schulenburg proved a dismal failure, disgracing his class and his profession by leaving the sinking ship in a hurry and by seeking refuge in the service of Napoleon's brother, the King of Westphalia.

The major steps in the professional advancement of Schulenburg-Kehnert epitomized the "ideal" sequence within the transformed pattern of bureaucratic career making, a progression which Frederick II came to love: noble squire of old family; army officer; *Landrat;* board president and, then, perhaps minister. Preferentially, appointment to top service rank was at an age not higher than thirty-five. By entrusting relatively numerous men of such background with directing positions, Frederick built, in the course of time, a junto of former *Landräte* and wellborn army officers within the bureaucratic nobility. Thus he brought about an internal regrouping of the leadership personnel, and he attempted to capitalize on this change by playing off the newcomers and the old-line regulars against each other. The professional and political upgrading of the squire-*Landräte* went

back to the late years of Frederick William
I. The new course really got under way
after "the soldiers' king" had made peace
with the Junkers, primarily through his
army reforms. The increased importance
of the *Landräte,* as a group, found expression in their promotion to a higher
grade in the service rank order and in the
extension of their functional prerogatives.

The *Landrat,* in the age of Frederick
II, was a part-time official who was
charged with manifold public responsibilities. He represented the central state
authority as a police chief, as a judicial
keeper of public peace and order, and as
a fiscal and military administrator. Part
of his job was to publicize royal edicts in
his district. He supervised the allocation
and transfer of direct taxes and the distribution of the heavy, service-extracting
military burdens imposed upon the popu-
lace. Accordingly, he took a hand, in cooperation with the regular military
authorities, in billeting troops, in exacting
military *corvées* such as transport services, and in personnel conscription for
the armed forces. He also was a surveyor
of the roads and the public utilities of his
county, and he interfered, through police
ordinances, in economic life.

As a rule, the *Landrat* was a particularly
prominent, economically independent
resident landowner and, very often, also
a former army officer, who came from an
old local family and received his appointment upon the nomination of the squires
of his county. There were exceptions to
this pattern, especially in the newly acquired provinces of Silesia and West
Prussia, largely Catholic, where the
landed nobility was reluctant to part with
its *Ständestaat* liberties through integration into the stern Prussian police and
garrison state. In these territories it was
customary to appoint the *Landrat* at will:
in Upper Silesia because of distrust in

the loyalty of the "Austrian-minded"
squires and in West Prussia for the sake
of getting the "Polish rabble" under control. In rare instances a freshly installed
Landrat, if he was a retired army officer
and utterly unprepared for his new job,
hired a substitute who did the work for
him and in return got part of his em-
ployer's salary.

In theory, the *Landrat's* official task was
to harmonize the objectives and activities
of the central government with those of
the local Junker landowners. In action,
he usually was loyal to his class and acted
as the trustee of the landed aristocracy,
without neglecting, however, his personal
affairs and self-interests. In many ways the
Prussian *Landrat* closely resembled the
English justice of the peace under the
Old Regime. The heavy influx of these
formidable guardians of the landed interest into the presidencies of the provincial centers of bureaucratic public
administration and into the central executive bodies in Berlin meant that the dynastic instruments of civil government
came to be operated largely by representatives of the squirearchy. Although
"representatives," in their new capacity
they changed, of necessity, their customary style of life and absorbed fresh
ideas. By becoming career bureaucrats
and top agents of absolute government
they were apt to develop, individually
and collectively, professional interests,
loyalties, and political ambitions which
were distinct from, though not necessarily
hostile to, those of their noble consti-
tuents.

In Frederick's Prussia, the "purified"
bureaucratic nobility was surrounded
by a number of checks designed to prevent it from acting independently. In
order to keep the bureaucracy in a state
of political bondage, Frederick put primary emphasis on his own vigilance. He

reserved to himself the supreme leadership and control of the administrative machine by pushing to the extreme autocratic direction from the cabinet, and by extending the employment of spies and informers. He introduced seasonal intimidation by means of his annual tours of inspection. But he clearly realized that personal safeguards of this kind were not enough to hold in subjection the royal servants who, he correctly assumed, "want to govern despotically, while their master is expected to be satisfied with the empty prerogative of issuing orders in his name." Hence Frederick also tried to curb the bureaucracy by a policy of making public administration by a single, unified group impossible. This he sought to accomplish by strengthening the position of established competing authorities; by breaking the central administration into many units; and by creating, through the medium of the *Régie*, a new rival authority.

Although almost all the newly appointed top bureaucrats now came from the old Junker ranks, Frederick also called upon the class of large landed proprietors, as such, to contain his own administrative service class. The landowning bureaucratic nobility and the nonbureaucratic landed nobility were similar and yet divergent groups. Contrary to the dominant political trend under Frederick William I, the administrative influence and political power of the squirearchy expanded in Frederickian Prussia.

Nowhere was dynastic absolutism as an operating political order a fixed and immovable system. Under the mighty impact of the immobilizing social forces of the pre-absolutist past, the rulers of the modernized dynastic state brought about, at the utmost, a limited broadening of the social base for recruiting governmental personnel and a rather superficial rationalization of state management by means of imperfectly centralized administrative and military *étatisme* and by shifting the foundation of public affairs from "private" to "public" law. This is the contribution which monarchical absolutism made to the transition from the medieval to the modern state. Nowhere did the evolution of the absolute system involve a steady growth of governmental centralism and of bureaucratization.

Frederick II encouraged the recrudescence of decentralizing tendencies, because he was deeply concerned about his political position as autocratic head of the state and because he came to fear the power of the royal servants. Therefore he sanctioned the reemergence of nonbureaucratic agencies of corporate self-government and a limited revival of the political influence of the noble landowners, as a group, in the affairs of the dynastic state. By supporting the natural foes of bureaucratic centralization and by promoting the reintroduction of elements of representative government, representative of the landed Junker interest, he sponsored, in effect, a partial restoration, though in altered forms, of the old territorial *Ständestaat*.

The political resurgence of the squirearchy led to several institutional adjustments and innovations. It began with the reconstruction of the *Regierungen* by Cocceji in cooperation with the provincial delegates of the landed aristocracy. Young Frederick supported the Lord Chancellor in his drive to put new life into the old official hierarchy to prevent thereby the new bureaucratic elite from becoming all-dominant in the manipulation of "nationalized" civil affairs. The concomitant upgrading of the *Landräte* was another phase of the royal policy of restraining the power of the regular bureaucracy.

A particularly noteworthy feature of Frederickian Prussia was the substantial regrowth of corporate-aristocratic home rule, functioning through the district assemblies of the noble landowners and through the committees which they elected. Through their activities in county government and administration the incoherent mass of privileged landholders was organized into cohesive local pressure groups. Through the *Landrat* and the memoranda which he submitted to the bureaucratic provincial boards, to individual ministers, to the General Directory, or to the King directly, the county associations of squires brought their reactions and thoughts to the attention of the central administration and obtained an indirect share in determining the direction and content of government policy and legislation.

Even on the provincial level, the squirearchy recovered some of its former vigor. It made its voice heard, especially after 1770 when it gained, with the aid of Frederick, a rallying center in the newly established *Landschaften*. These institutions which did so much to foster the growth of agricultural production and the improvement of farming methods and estate management under the leadership of daring Junker entrepreneurs were not vested, in the formal sense, with any political function, let alone authority. Technically, they were merely provincial mortgage credit societies created for the purpose of ensuring a common economic advantage to their members through collective self-help and compulsory joint liability. In practice, however, the directors and members of these incorporated bodies of large landowners and capital investors did not hold "politics" in contempt. The meetings of the elected board of directors *(Landschaftsräte)* lent themselves to the free exchange of information, opinions, and ideas and to the formulation of petitions, requests, and complaints, "respectfully submitted" to the central government. In matters of state legislation, the *Landschaften* frequently functioned as consultative agencies. Through formal and informal channels, they also brought pressure to bear upon ranking officials of their province who administered the government's economic, social, and fiscal policies.

The landed aristocracy of the two provinces of West and East Prussia, however, had to wait for Frederick's death to be blessed with a *Landschaft*. In West Prussia, most of the land belonged to Polish noblemen and, as it were, the king held a poor opinion of the "dissolute Polish trash." And as for East Prussia, Frederick never forgot and never forgave his noble "vassals" for the fact that many of them, during the ordeal of the Seven Years' War, had shown a kind of "esprit de corps et de nation" which made them "Russian- rather than Prussian-minded and, moreover, capable of all those infamies of which one accuses the Poles."

In his search for effective methods of keeping the royal servants in their allotted place, Frederick ventured to underpin administrative and political "deconcentration" by dismantling, in part, the service apparatus of the central government itself. He curtailed the managerial jurisdictions of the collegiate General Directory, weakened its unity, and dissolved its joint responsibility and collective solidarity by means of organizational manipulations. He created new functional ministries, only nominally connected with the Directory which hitherto had been the supreme body of central administration. Thus between 1741 and 1770, he established special central departments for trade and industry, for the army, for mining and smelting, and for forestry, under single ministers directly responsible to him. He also instituted a separate administration for Silesia under a special minister who, residing in Breslau [Wroctaw] was completely independent from the General Directory. Frequently, Frederick bypassed the Directory and also the other central agencies by giving orders directly to prominent members of the provincial and local administration or by appointing special commissars for special tasks. By founding the *Régie,* in 1776, he dealt a heavy blow to the permanent civil bureaucracy as a whole. This reorganization meant that the direction of the entire administration of the indirect taxes and of the customs duties and, for a few years, also of the postal service was turned over to a small group of French fiscal experts who at first were given a free hand in building up their own central, provincial, and local staff. These immigrants formed a privileged category of special royal servants. They received exceptionally high salaries, and they functioned as "public entrepreneurs," entitled to engage in private profiteering by appropriating 5 per cent of all revenues collected in excess of the stipulated minimum.

The "newest of the new bureaucrats" were headed by de Launay who, next to Frederick himself, was the most powerful man in the civil administration of Prussia during the two decades from 1766 to 1786. The royal leader had meant to go even further. Frederick had intended to entrust the French reformers also with the management of the crown's timber resources and of the tobacco and salt monopolies. Moreover, he had wanted to "debureaucratize" this whole bundle of "nationalized" fiscal prerogatives by farming them out on a strictly commer-

cial basis. Aware of the risks, de Launay declined this generous offer. Thus he won a noteworthy battle for the regular Prussian bureaucracy which nonetheless regarded him as a most undesirable enemy alien.

By the introduction of the *Régie,* the traditional bureaucrats temporarily lost a large part of their managerial dominion and a major source of their perquisites. Through the rival authority of the *Régie,* the whole civil state bureaucracy was split wide open and converted into two implacably hostile organizations. Thus, just after the century-old conflict between the old and the new official hierarchies had been reconciled, a far more bitter service dualism developed which could not be resolved by compromise. Thereafter, the administrative manager class was an unforgiving and remorseless opponent of the new fiscal bureaucrats. In consequence, it was prepared, more than ever before, to close ranks with the high judiciary against the common enemy: the officials of the *Régie* and the trouble maker behind them, the bullying "royal master."

"Power controlled or abridged," as Alexander Hamilton once remarked, "is almost always the rival and enemy of that power by which it is controlled or abridged."[3] Distrustful political competition and increasing antagonism rather than harmonious cooperation marked the relations between personal autocracy and collective bureaucracy in Frederickian Prussia. The royal servants refused to function as obedient, spineless human instruments in the hands of the obstinate monarch. The tortuous policy of containing the bureaucracy sprang from the inane, false, and frightening idea which Frederick II had throughout harbored

---

[3] *The Federalist or the New Constitution* (Everyman's Library), 72.

in his mind, the idea that all Prussian subjects, including "l'élite de la nation," could be kept in motion like machines by the royal chief engineer.

Frederick continued to play the central role as the initiator and maker of state policy and as the chief supervisor of the enforcement of laws and policy, but most of the checks and balances with which he surrounded his administrators boomeranged. As a matter of fact, the bureaucratic elite managed to gain a high degree of liberty from royal restraints and to exact retribution for being treated contemptuously and, as a rule, disrespectfully. Its members did not rest content with the routine job of executing official directives, cabinet orders, and predetermined policies. They effectively contrived to usurp if not the right then at least the practice of codetermining government policy and of blocking the enforcement of royal regulations and decisions if they saw fit to do so. Like the French *noblesse de robe,* the Prussian bureaucratic nobility, in moving against the absolute monarch, acted in accordance with the thought "that it could successfully overcome all the opposition he could put out in action, and in due time make his authority secondary to its own."[4]

The real power of the Prussian Crown gradually declined during the second half of the eighteenth century. The formal transformation of monarchical autocracy into a system of bureaucratic-aristocratic authoritarianism, as effected in 1807 and 1808, legalized and reinforced this political development. In the reconstructed Old Regime, as it emerged from the increasingly enlightened late eighteenth century, political leadership and the responsibility for high level policy making were concentrated in the ministerial chiefs of the civil bureaucracy which preserved the tradition of paternal government by dictation. The Junker historian Theodor von der Goltz, writing at a much later time and arguing in terms of *"Realpolitik,"* understated his case when he proudly noted that the Hohenzollerns in the age of absolutism, though nominally equipped with "unlimited power," had, in reality, to rely "chiefly on their noble companions as advisers and executive organs and were compelled to take into account their opinions, desires, and frame of mind."[5]

Diverse forces brought about the transmutation of the "royal servants" into a self-governing professional corporation and a policy and law making political oligarchy.

---

[4] *The Memoirs of the Duke of Saint-Simon,* II (New York, 1936), part IV.

[5] Theodor Freiherr von der Goltz, *Geschichte der deutschen Landwirtschaft,* II (Stuttgart, 1903), 165–66.

GERHARD SCHILFERT is professor of modern
history and director of the Institute of General History
at Humboldt University in East Berlin. His first major
scholarly interest was the abortive universal suffrage
movement of 1848–1849. Recently he has entered the
international debate over the "crisis of early
capitalism."[1] The following pages are drawn from a
textbook he wrote for the unitary series published by
the "popularly owned" *(volkseigener Betrieb)* East
German Scientific Press. It may be useful to compare
his sometimes rhetorical argumentation with
Rosenberg's application of the materialist outlook.[*]

Gerhard Schilfert

Junker Militarism:
An East German View

Enlightened Despotism as a historical phenomenon rests upon . . . the progress of productive forces and their social consequences. But it would have been inconceivable without the cultural attainments of the bourgeoisie, which had a permanent influence on state life. Furthermore, a series of princes and statesmen were influenced by the Age of Reason. The spread of the bourgeois Enlightenment along with the acceleration of capitalistic manufactories contributed to a shift in the attitude of the feudal superstructure,[2]

especially with respect to political institutions. Another major factor was the mounting antifeudal movement and the opposition of the masses, as expressed in rebellions of peasants, apprentices, and miners.

Since the already declining feudal class could no longer hope to forestall bourgeois development by force alone and expected the worst of a united opposition of burghers and peasants, it strove, up to a point, to make its superstructure

[1] Gerhard Schilfert, "Die Revolutionen beim Übergang vom Feudalismus zum Kapitalismus," *Zeitschrift für Geschichtswissenschaft,* XVII (1969), 171–193. A paper presented at the Fourth Congress of Historians of the German Democratic Republic.

[2] Marxist writers understand the word "feudal"

to mean primarily a *social* system based upon manorial land-tenure relationships. Western historians, implicitly rejecting economic determinism, prefer to use this adjective to designate a system of *political* and *governmental* relationships (of which manorialism was a subordinate feature) such as existed in the Central Middle Ages.—Ed.

[*]From Gerhard Schilfert, *Deutschland: 1648–1789,* "Lehrbuch der deutschen Geschichte (Beiträge)" (Berlin: VEB Deutscher Verlag der Wissenschaften, 1962), pp. 156–158, 160–168, 172–176, 181. Translated by Thomas M. Barker.

acceptable to the middle class. The absolutist state found it expedient to make concessions. . . . It sought to appear as "Enlightened" as possible, but in reality it preserved its basic character unchanged. The fact that in many places in Germany bourgeois elements permitted themselves to be won over on a broad basis by concessions to their ideology, or rather took the latter at face value, shows the weakness of capitalistic development in the country. Such utterances as "the ruler is the first servant of the state" or "the monarch must work only for the common good" altered not even a little the fundamental fact that from start to finish the Enlightenment was and remained an instrument of the feudal class for the oppression of other classes. . . . Because the bourgeoisie, as represented by its leading figures, often succumbed to such false conceptions and generally gave in to the illusion of a peaceful transition from the feudal to the bourgeois state order, the evolution of the necessary preconditions for a bourgeois revolution in Germany became all the more difficult. . . .

If one considers the situation in Prussia on the death of Frederick William I superficially, it might appear at first as if the Junker state could have taken on the traits of the bourgeois Enlightenment. Many contemporaries expected innovations of this kind from the new ruler, but the objective socioeconomic conditions were not yet sufficiently mature for such a development. . . . According to observers of the day, there were signs that Frederick, already subject to the influence of the rationalists, would follow in practice the principles he had imbibed. The new ideas of the Enlightenment, above all in its French manifestation, were already so prevalent that not even princely states could escape their spell entirely.

These ideas made themselves felt particularly in the education of heirs to the throne, which in Germany as elsewhere was much affected by France. . . . On his accession Frederick agreed to certain measures—individually of some significance but leaving the basic features of the state unchanged—which reflected the Enlightenment. Among them, for example, was the abolition of torture as well as other improvements in the administration of justice, the reestablishment of the Academy of Sciences, the declaration of tolerance, and a temporary freedom of press. However, despite Frederick's predilection for the Enlightenment, the raison d'état of the Junker state, which he had learned to respect thoroughly during his youth, was from the start the law that governed his actions. Walther Hubatsch is entirely unjustified in citing the maxim "everybody for the sake of everybody" as the basic principle of the Prussian state and in asserting that the ideals of the Enlightenment were not necessarily in conflict with Staatsräson.[3] Prussian raison d'état and the objectives of the Enlightenment were mutually exclusive as the respective ideologies of the noble and burgher classes. . . . The military character of the Prussian state, which had fully matured already under King Frederick William I, became all the more distinctive under Frederick II. The latter immediately strengthened the army, and at the first favorable opportunity (afforded by the death of Emperor Charles VI) unleashed an aggressive war in order to rob Austria of Silesia. . . .

The permanent strain of maintaining the new acquisition became a heavy burden for the Prussian people, especially

---

[3] Walther Hubatsch, Das Problem der Staatsräson bei Friedrich dem Grossen (Göttingen, 1956), p. 21.

the workers and peasants, who were the ones to suffer most from the whole state's having become "an armed camp in the middle of peace." A characteristic example of this state of affairs is the growth of poverty in the cities of the Electoral March, where between 1750 and 1810 there was a ninefold increase in the number of paupers. A series of uprisings by workers and apprentices also provide evidence of the unfavorable situation. For example, in 1761 unrest broke out among the Berlin clothmaking apprentices and in 1786 among the local lacemakers.

The kind of conditions which existed in the army is shown by the fact that in Berlin between 1781 and 1786 there was one suicide for every thousand civilians but four for every hundred soldiers. The exacerbation of militarism along with constant preparation for war created a unique situation for the oppressed classes: Lessing was moved to call Prussia "the most enslaved land of Europe." This system, to which the whole life of the people was subject, served only to maintain and strengthen Junker rule. It could not be justified on the basis of national necessity. Indeed, just the opposite was true, for "there thus arose in Germany, alongside the Emperor, an adversary who was almost equal in rank and who made the division of the country rigid and permanent" (Friedrich Engels). In the last analysis only military considerations were crucial for the state of Frederick II. The economic demands of war were determinative already in peacetime. The King strove constantly to exploit to the highest possible degree not only the human but also the material resources of the land. Nowhere in Europe was the economy so harnessed to the service of the state. Thus the production of consumer goods for the nonnoble population

was sharply curtailed. Frederick II stifled the criticism against his military fiscal policies which was leveled at the beginning of the reign by bourgeois merchants and entrepreneurs. Although he demanded maximal productive achievement from factories, he spent for their encouragment only a fraction of the amount that he lavished upon the army. Alongside luxury manufactories which worked only to supply the prestige needs of the Court and the nobility, the most privileged enterprises were those that produced weapons and uniforms. The so-called "workers' colonies and spinners' villages," made up mostly of foreigners, were generally involved in this activity. The workers were subject to the most gruesome kind of forced labor, and the last drop of sweat was squeezed from their brows.

It may therefore be said that workers and peasants were equally oppressed. Even the Silesian peasants, who had just come under Prussian rule, had to give the state about 34 percent of their income. Frederick II not only continued the political practices of his father, but, in fact, brought military despotism to its culmination insofar as he promoted the warlike Junker class. Thus the old administrative apparatus remained untouched. . . . In contrast to his father, Frederick had only one bourgeois minister, and he sought, as a matter of principle, to keep bourgeois officials out of his office as much as possible. He dealt with his ministers only in writing and received them only occasionally. He carried on all current state business with the aid of his personal cabinet, whose members were supposed to be nothing more than tools. Of course, these so-called "cabinet councillors" frequently knew more about the most important state affairs than did the ministers. Since they were also made privy to all state secrets, they were indispensable to the King. At his command they maintained a special intelligence and informer service, and so they learned of important developments before they were known to the ministers.

Not only the overall character of the Prussian state but also the style of Frederick's government had features contrary to the aims of the Enlightenment, for both were the expression of the effort by the declining feudal class to maintain a position of power with the surest means available. The Enlightened aspect of Frederick's militaristic-bureaucratic despotism may be compared with a beautiful facade, which, to be sure, deceived many an important representative of bourgeois ideology, at least initially. It is significant that it was mainly Frenchmen who let themselves be taken in by Frederick's Gallic education. . . . As ideologists of a country with progressive social relationships and a highly developed national consciousness, they turned their attention chiefly to his French speeches and writings and not to his feudal-reactionary state practices, which were difficult for them to comprehend. They hardly noted the contradictions between his words and his actions, as did the German rationalists, particularly Lessing. . . .

To judge by his own utterances and declarations, Frederick's policies were aimed to achieve the well-being of all inhabitants of the state, and he regarded his highest duty as consisting in exhausting service to the collective social body. Many nationalist historians have accepted such words all too gladly and willingly and have lauded Frederick II as a hero who consumed himself in devoted labor for the commonweal and thus as the exemplary Enlightenment monarch. . . . But one must judge a personality and a

régime not by its words but by its deeds, which in the case of Frederick happened to serve definite class interests, that is, those of the Junkers. That Frederick's confession of Enlightened faith had no practical meaning is demonstrated by the fact that as a *philosophe* he was an advocate of the bourgeois contract theory of government and of equality but as a statesman he consciously favored the nobility. In this he also distinguished himself from his father, who of course took no notice of such bourgeois doctrines yet objectively furthered the interests of the middle class more than did his successor. Indicative of Frederick's true view of the Enlightenment is his saying, "To desire to enlighten mankind is love's labor lost; indeed it is often a hazardous enterprise. One must be satisfied with being wise when one can be, and one must leave the common herd to its erroneous ways, seeking only to prevent it from committing crimes which disturb the social order." Frederick II regarded serfdom as despicable. Yet in practice he condescended to only a few energetic attempts to abolish it, although breaking the resistance of the nobility would certainly have been easier for him than for his predecessor. Although by his own words he regarded "high birth as only a chimera," he presumed as a matter of natural fact that the nobility had a higher sense of honor than the *roturiers,* whom he scorned. The nobility knew that the state which he so ambitiously served was *not* a state in which everything was done for the people but one in which, practically speaking, the supreme commandment was maintenance of the prerogatives and underpinnings of aristocracy. An evaluation based upon the theory of class politics shows that the Prussian state merely supported with newfangled means the most intrinsic cause of the nobility. Only as a consequence of the generally growing weakness of the decadent feudal class was the state forced to justify the nobles' existence in a language understandable to the ascendant bourgeoisie. Here, too, one may discern the prime social reason for the contradiction between the *philosophe* Frederick, who loved to associate with the most august bourgeois minds of Europe, and the politician, who fended off meritorious bourgeois statesmen and officers. The dichotomy which frequently exists in Frederick between theory and practice may thus be traced back to objective grounds and not to any taste for hyprocrisy or other subjective personal traits. In the last analysis, then, the "Enlightened" aspect of Frederick is the subjective expression of the objective status of the feudal class, which could no longer hope to keep its power intact in its period of decline without certain limited concessions to the bourgeoisie. These concessions were restricted or ceased entirely as soon as an essential class interest of the Junkers was affected. Thus, as the representative of this group, Frederick II yielded only a little in filling important state offices with bourgeois officials, whereas in the realm of cultural policy he proved to be much more obliging. Furthermore, when, to use Lessing's phrase, he tolerated "carrying as many stupidities against religion into the market place as one wishes," it was simply the expression of the fact that ecclesiastical orthodoxy had ceased to be the main ideological support of the feudal class. Why shouldn't it be possible, without any worry, to leave the opponents of orthodoxy in peace as long as they did not question the God-given right of the nobility to leadership?

Since the whole legal system of the Prussian state was oriented to the vital requirements of the feudal class . . . , in individual cases it was not particularly difficult to favor the Junkers. Within this given framework many Enlightenment doctrines were adapted to the system of justice, and thus in comparison with previous decades important improvements were effected. Through Cocceji's reform program, later continued by Carmer and Suarez, certain former evils, such as unduly extended trials, were overcome. However, in comparison with the army and other aspects of state life, legal administration was treated in no less stepmotherly a way than education. To be sure, Frederick did not deal with the Academy of Sciences as shamefully as his father, but the many abuses in the school system were hardly touched. Although the "General School Ordinance" of 1763 required "exercising the intellect of youth," the goal was seldom achieved because school jobs served as sinecures for veterans who took care that such "exercise" remained within the limits set by the Junker state. . . .

In order to combat the adverse effects of the Seven Years' War, reconstruction, the *"Rétablissement"* as it was then called, was undertaken in all territories that had suffered. Whereas bourgeois development was furthered by a concurrent program in Saxony and certain permanent alleviations were accorded its population, the burden on the Prussian people remained the same. The claim that Frederick, like a kind father of his country, healed the wounds inflicted upon it in wartime is thus a legend. . . . The financial resources appropriated for rehabilitation were slight in relation to army costs and appropriations for the construction of great palaces as, for example, the Neue Palais in Potsdam, begun immediately after the war. Almost nothing was done for the pitiful victims of the recent con-

flict, the invalid soldiers. In fact, in order
to be free of them, the Prussian state went
so far as to grant them the permission to
beg as a kind of old-age pension, and so
the number of mendicants increased
greatly. The King's most pressing concern
was that the army "might arise from the
ashes like a phoenix." After only four
years it was strengthened anew, although
discharges at the conclusion of peace and
increased employment of settlers had not
sufficed to satisfy the needs of the labor
force. The army grew more rapidly than
the population at large. . . . The peasants
had to provide the money for reconstruction, but although they had been the most
affected by the war, they derived far less
benefit from it than did the nobility.
Indeed, the pressure on the peasant
masses subject to the Junkers only increased. The lot of the peasants on crown
land was the only case of improvement.

Frederick II's reforms on the Royal
Demesnes were in no way dictated by
solicitude for peasant welfare. To be sure,
freshly revived plans for hereditary
tenancy were no longer as much motivated by pressure to increase state revenues as in the days of Frederick William
I. Yet the goal was once more to
strengthen the Prussian Junker state.
In renting a number of Demesnal farms
hereditarily, Frederick desired above
all to employ efficient tenants. Thus the
labor force was augmented, agrarian
production (which hereditary tenants
were more inclined to promote as compared with serfs) mounted, and the
domestic market was stimulated. Hence,
in the last analysis, income expanded
even if the growth came about indirectly.
Although the situation of some Demesnal
peasants themselves also was improved,
hereditary tenancy under Frederick II
was still unable to evolve into an institu-
tion that could shake the foundations of
feudal productive relationships. To what
extent hereditary tenancy continued
subject to the interests of maintaining
Junker power is shown by the circum-
stance that feudal ties of dependency
generally remained in effect for many
peasants who, for example, still had to
render personal services. Thus the partial
introduction of hereditary tenancy into
Prussia in the decades after 1763 brought
about no fundamental alteration in the
system of the Second Enserfment.[4] That
conflicts with the nobility over the abolition of serfdom were no more than feints
is proved, among other things, by the
rather vaguely formulated royal ordinance of 1763 and the response thereto
by the Pomeranian Estates. . . .

Even Frederick's entire so-called
"peasant safeguard policy," which has
been incorrectly praised by many historians . . . , was in the overall interest
of the Junker state. It was based upon a
cool calculation of state advantage. By
means of the so-called "Prohibitions and
Restrictions Concerning the Enclosure of
Peasant Holdings" [Bauernlegenverbote],
it was not the individual peasants who
were protected but rather the total number of farmsteads. Existing units were to
be preserved: that is, insofar as certain
peasants were expropriated, their positions did not need to be filled by the same
persons but could be occupied by others.
Thus, more than anything else, a loss in
tax revenue could be prevented. The preservation of a minimum number of places
was likewise imperative because of the

---

[4] This is a term with which Communist historians
describe the reversion of the East European peasantry to a status of personal dependency in Early
Modern times. This development was caused in part
by the import demands of the more advanced,
capitalistic Western European economy for agricultural commodities and the resultant need of
profit-minded manorial lords for cheap and easily
controlled labor. — Ed.

need to supply recruits, furnish victuals and fodder, and provide quartering. In this case, as generally, Frederick was smarter than the Junkers. The latter often raised a great hue and cry over royal ordinances which in practice were frequently ignored. The nobles were so shortsighted that they could not see that these ostensibly propeasant edicts lay directly in the overall interest of preserving feudal state institutions. The decrees would have been detrimental to the aristocracy only if bourgeois capital had entered into the peasant economy simultaneously. However, this was exactly what Frederick's measures prevented. Indeed, they buttressed the power of the feudal class at a crucial point. In the same context one must mention the distinct disadvantages imposed upon bourgeois landowners, who, *inter alia,* might not exercise patrimonial jurisdiction or advowson and hunting rights. Likewise they were not allowed any voice in electing the district magistrate. Further acquisition of noble property (directed mainly against the Polish nobility), with few exceptions, was also forbidden in order to prevent the penetration of newly wealthy burghers into the caste of large estate owners.

Above all else Frederick II concerned himself after 1763 with the heavy indebtedness of noble property, especially in Silesia. It was therefore also here that he first created the so-called "Provincial Associations" *(Landschaften).* These were credit institutions that advanced money to noble property owners at low interest rates, the cash deriving mainly from urban lenders. The latter were permitted to deal only with the Association, not with the individual creditors, and thus the latter were quite broadly protected. . . . Taken all together, these factors furthered the growth of prerequi-

sites for the later development of agricultural capitalism, in which Junkerdom remained dominant. . . .

During the Seven Years' War some of the Prussian bourgeoisie, especially in Berlin, were able to engage in profitable business, in part because of army contracts. At the same time they came into frequent contact with foreign capitalists, particularly the Dutch. Prussian merchants were accordingly all the more involved in a credit and exchange crisis which spread from the Netherlands to Berlin via Hamburg. As a result of the bankruptcy of the most important trading and entrepreneurial houses, the economy was seriously harmed. . . . The tobacco and (later) coffee monopoly, the rise in the excise tax, and the establishment of privileged trading companies may be seen in retrospect as characteristic of a backward economic policy. . . . These monopolies and imposts were part of the continuing effort to provide large financial resources for the army by imposing fresh sacrifices upon the people, the object of which was to deter Prussia's opponents, especially Austria, from seeking revenge for the theft of Silesia. Thus Prussia's policy of larceny and the desire of its adversaries to square accounts were factors that contributed to an economic burdening of the bourgeoisie far heavier than was the case in other states. . . .

The trading companies increased the price of wool, the raw material most essential to the economy. The Prussian Bank, established in 1765, put merchants under such extreme pressure that their credit status abroad suffered. There were also high transit duties. All these measures hindered further economic development considerably and aroused strong opposition in many bourgeois circles. . . . When in 1766 the Directorate General advocated the encouragement of bourgeois economic interests, at least in certain respects, on the basis of a plan devised by the distinguished Privy Economic Councillor Ursinus, Frederick reacted against the implied criticism most cruelly. Ursinus, a victim of the reactionary Junker *Staatsräson* of Prussia,[5] was dismissed and taken to the fortress. . . . It is also indicative that on several occasions the King forced the owners of big capital to invest their funds industrially where *he* thought it expedient. The degree to which commercial policy was basically detrimental to the progress-minded bourgeoisie is evident from the fact that high duties for the products of Prussia's Rhenine territories remained in effect. As a whole the economic policy of Frederick the Great, especially in comparison with that of other German states (above all Saxony and Berlin), scarcely redounds to his glory. . . . By clinging to mercantilistic principles long after they had

outlived themselves he . . . restrained, rather than encouraged, the growth and impetus of manufactories. . . .

Fate was unkind to German history. Precisely in the state which became, by systematic exploitation of all resources and by unprecedentedly harsh discipline, the only German political entity apart from Austria to attain great-power status, the growing strength of the people was tightly bridled. Likewise between 1648 and 1789 Prussia heavily encumbered the relationship of the German people with its neighbors. The brutal policy of suppression *vis-à-vis* the Poles deserves particular mention. It was a misfortune for Germany and for adjacent nations that with eighteenth-century Prussia there arose to European prominence a state whose dominant class was able to maintain its position only be means of particularly intense social and national oppression. . . . Above and beyond this, Frederick's government contributed to the ability of the Junker class to keep itself in power well into the twentieth century to the greatest detriment of Germany and of the world.

---

[5] Marxists consider this phenomenon "reactionary" (in contrast to "progressive") because it was opposed to the basic nature of the historical process as viewed by Communism, that is, dialectical materialism or the sequential system of struggle by one class against exploitation by another. — Ed.

Suggestions for Further Reading

It is impossible to list all the titles pertaining to Frederick the Great in so restricted a space. The material, if not quite as bulky as that dealing with Napoleon, is still very extensive. Therefore the following references should be considered a somewhat arbitrary selection. In addition to using the bibliographical aids, the student should consult the most recent issues of *Historische Zeitschrift.*

Bibliographical Aids Pierre Gaxotte, *Frederick the Great* (London, 1941), pp. 397–410. Walther Hubatsch, *Das Zeitalter des Absolutismus,* 2d ed., (Braunschweig, 1965), pp. 247–249, 250–251.

Source Collections and Memoires R. Koser, G. B. Volz (eds.), *Politische Korrespondenz Friedrichs des Grossen,* 46 vols. (Berlin, 1877–1939). R. Koser (ed.), *Unterhaltungen mit Friedrich dem Grossen* (Leipzig, 1884); De Catt's recollections (in French). J. P. E. Preuss (ed.), *Oeuvres de Frédéric le Grand,* 30 vols. (Decker, 1846–1857); textually insufficient and must be supplemented with *Politische Korrespondenz.* J. Richter, *Die Briefe Friedrichs des Grossen an seinen vormaligen Kammerdiener Fredersdorf* (Berlin, 1926); Frederick's presumptive love life. Dieudonné Thiébault, *Original Anecdotes of Frederick the Second,* 2 vols. (London, 1805); memoirs of an intellectual associate. François Marie Arouet Voltaire, *Mémoires pour servir à la vie de M. de Voltaire,* (Paris, 1965); to be used with caution; also Voltaire, *Vie privée du roi de Prusse* (Paris, 1759); the same applies. Wilhelmine, Margravine of Bayreuth, *Mémoires* (London, 1812); Frederick's favorite sister. G. B. Volz, *Die politischen Testamente Friedrichs des Grossen* (Berlin, 1920); essential supplement to the *Politische Korrespondenz.* G. B. Volz, F. von Oppeln-Bronikowski, *Friedrich der Grosse und Wilhelmine von Bayreuth,* 2 vols. (Leipzig, 1894); German translation of correspondence; French originals unpublished. Dr. Zimmerman, *Conversations with the Late King of Prussia* (London, 1791); deathbed discussions with the attendant physician.

Historiography Karl Erich Born, *Der Wandel des Friedrichbildes in Deutschland während des 19. Jahrhunderts* (Cologne, 1953). Walter Bussmann, "Friedrich der Grosse im Wandel des europäischen Urteils" in Werner Conze (ed.), *Deutschland und Europa: historische Studien zur Völker- und Staatenordnung des Abendlandes* ("Festschrift für Hans Rothfels zum 60. Geburtstag am 12. April 1951") (Düsseldorf, 1951). Stephan Skalweit, "Das Problem von Recht und Macht und das historiographische Bild Friedrich des Grossen" in *Geschichte in Wissenschaft und Unterricht,* II (1951), 91–106.

Older or Historiographically Significant Accounts Duc de Broglie, *Frédéric II et Marie Thérèse* (Paris, 1871). Thomas Carlyle, *History of Frederick II of Prussia, called Frederick the Great,* 10 vols. (London, 1872–1873); a good personal portrait but otherwise outdated. Johann Gustaf Droysen, *Geschichte der preussischen Politik,* 5 vols. (Leipzig, 1868–1880); a classic representing the Little German viewpoint. Oskar Fritsch, *Friedrich der Grosse, unser Held und Führer* (Munich, 1936); Nazi outlook. Onno Klopp, *Frédéric II, Roi de Prusse, et la Nature Allemande* (Brussels, 1866); the hostile account of a Hannoverian patriot. R. F. Kaindl, *Österreich,*

101

Preussen, Deutschland: deutsche Geschichte in grossdeutscher Beleuchtung (Vienna, 1926); hostile Austro-German nationalist viewpoint.

Thomas Babington Macaulay (first baron), *Life of Frederick the Great* (New York, 1865); somewhat disapproving of Frederick on the basis of liberal value judgment. Jules Michelet, *Histoire de France,* vol. 16 (Paris, 1866), pp. 170, 409–421; adulatory; written before the Franco-Prussian War. Franz Mehring, *Die Lessing Legende* (Stuttgart, 1893); classical Marxist view; exculpates Frederick as tool of historical laws. Leopold von Ranke, "Friedrich der Zweite, König von Preussen," *Werke,* vol. 5 (Leipzig, 1888); a politically conservative viewpoint; sees Frederick's goal as party with Austria and approves of German "Dualism." William F. Reddaway, *Frederick the Great and the Rise of Prussia* (New York, 1904); a straightforward somewhat uncritical account, stressing the successful aggrandizement of Prussia. Heinrich von Treitschke, *The Confessions of Frederick the Great, King of Prussia and the Life of Frederick the Great* (London, 1914); extreme German nationalist viewpoint.

General Willy Andreas, "Friedrich der Grosse, der siebenjährige Krieg und der Hubertusburger Friede," *Historische Zeitschrift,* CLVIII (1938), 170–178. W. H. Bruford, "The Origin and Rise of Prussia," *New Cambridge Modern History,* vol. 7, (London, 1957), pp. 292–317. W. Dilthey, "Friedrich der Grosse und die deutsche Aufklärung," *Gesammelte Schriften,* vol. 3 (Berlin, 1927); for Frederick's relationship to German Enlightenment. W. L. Dorn, "The Prussian Bureaucracy in the Eighteenth Century," *Political Science Quarterly,* XLVI (1931), 402–423; XLVII (1932), 75–94, 259–273; a case study on the local level. Chester Easum, *Prince Henry of Prussia,* (Madison, Wis., 1942); a massive scholarly effort. Walter Eltze, *Friedrich der Grosse, geistige Welt, Schicksal, Taten* (Berlin, 1936); good battle maps. Robert Ergang, *The Potsdam Führer* (New York, 1941); a study of Frederick William I. O. Groehler, *Die Kriege Friedrichs II* (Berlin, 1966); a fine technical study set within the East German ideological framework.
Fritz Hartung, "Der aufgeklärte Absolutis-

mus," *Historische Zeitschrift,* CLXXX (1955), 26–31; also translated excerpts ("The Typical Enlightened Despot") in Roger Wine, *Enlightened Despotism,* "Problems in European Civilization" (Boston, 1967) pp. 28–31; sees Frederick as a combination of Enlightenment influences and the historical tradition of Absolutism. Also Hartung, *Deutsche Verfassungen vom 15. Jahrhundert bis zur Gegenwart* (Leipzig-Berlin, 1922); constitutional background. Ludwig Häusser, *Deutsche Geschichte vom Tode Friedrich des Grossen bis zur Gründung des Deutschen Bundes,* 4 vols. (Berlin, 1869). W. O. Henderson, *Studies in the Economic Policy of Frederick the Great* (London, 1963); an analysis of Frederick's energetic mercantilism. Carl Hinrichs, *Der Kronprinzenprozess, Friedrich und Kathe* (Berlin, 1936); Frederick's trial of 1730 with documents. Otto Hintze, *Preussische Verfassungs-, Verwaltungs- und Finanzgeschichte* (Berlin, 1921); for constitutional, administrative, and fiscal background.

Leonard Krieger, *The German Idea of Freedom* (Boston, 1957); Frederick's role in the development of the authoritarian mentality in Germany. Werner Langer, "Friedrich der Grosse und die geistige Welt Frankreichs," vol. 11, *Hamburger Studien zu Volkstum und Kultur der Romanen* (Hamburg, 1932); Frederick and the French Enlightenment. Max Lehmann, *Friedrich der Grosse und der Ursprung des Siebenjährigen Krieges* (Leipzig, 1894); places blame on Frederick for outbreak of Seven Years' War, then starting another historical debate. J. Luvaas, ed., *Frederick the Great on the Art of War* (New York: Free Press, 1966). Le Comte de Mirabeau, *De la monarchie prussienne,* 7 vols. (London, 1788); a still important contemporary analysis. Nancy Mitford, *Frederick the Great* (New York, 1970), lavishly illustrated, delightfully written but superficial. A. Naudel, *Beiträge zur Entstehungsgeschichte des Siebenjährigen Krieges,* 2 vols. (Leipzig, 1895–1896); continuation of discussion over "war guilt question." L. Paul-Dubois, *Frédéric le Grand d'après sa correspondance politique* (Paris, 1903); best French study between Lavisse and Gaxotte.

Gustav Schmoller, *The Mercantile System and Its Historical Significance* (New York, 1931); Frederick's economic policy. G. Schmoller, O. Hintze, E. Posner, (eds.), *Die Behördenorganisation und die allgemeine Staatsverwaltung,* 13 vols. (Berlin, 1894–1937); a part of the gigantic series "Acta Borussica"; treats the bureaucracy. Edith Simon, *The Making of Frederick the Great* (London, 1963); a readable, popular account of the year 1745. Lytton Strachey, "Voltaire and Frederick the Great," *Books and Character, French and English* (New York, 1922); the relationship between Frederick and Voltaire as seen from the particular viewpoint of the Bloomsbury Circle. Ludwig Tümpel, *Die Entstehung des brandenburgisch-preussischen Einheitsstaates im Zeitalter des Absolutismus 1609–1806;* the study of the development of the Prussian war. Frederick Veale, *Frederick the Great* (London, 1935); a serviceable general account but historically critical. Hermann Weil, *Frederick the Great and Samuel von Cocceji: A Study in the Reform of the Prussian Judicial Administration, 1740–1755* (Madison, Wis., 1967). Constance Wright, *A Royal Affinity: the Study of Frederick the Great and His Sister, Wilhelmine of Bayreuth* (New York, 1965); a popular biography based on thorough research.